Cosplay DIY Workbook

Fundamentals of Low-Sew and No-Sew **Costume Making**

by Pattie Wilkinson

LEISURE ARTS, INC. • Maumelle, Arkansas

Meet the Author

For Pattie Wilkinson, growing up as a minister's daughter in Oklahoma meant that being frugal and making something from nothing was more the rule than the exception. And that's how her creative lifestyle began. Known to her friends as "Pattiewack," Pattie made her first costume from an old bedsheet when playing the character Annie in a grade-school rendition of the musical *Annie Get Your Gun*. She was always in the middle of her mom's sewing and craft projects and remembers using washcloths to make house shoes for seniors at the local nursing home.

From that creative spark in her childhood, Pattie has blossomed into a DIY guru who takes joy in making anything from dumpster-diving projects to runway couture, and sometimes both at the same time. You could say her style is the love child of Betsey Johnson and Bill Nye the Science Guy! According to the ***Santa Paula Times*** newspaper, "She's wild, she's wacky and she's got a million ideas to transform the humdrum into wow, bring new life to everyday objects, or create something that is both out of this world and daringly stylish."

Pattie has accumulated more than 25 years of experience globally as a designer, consultant, media personality, video producer, author, inventor, content curator, licensee, and new product development manager. She hosted how-to videos for LifetimeTV.com, appeared as a guest on the networks DIY, QVC, HSN,

ABC, and cohosted the weekday craft show *Aleene's Creative Living* on TNN.

Pattie's love of glue and mixed media art led her to write *The Crafter's Guide to Glue*. In addition, she's written hundreds of editorials, project sheets, booklets, and blog posts throughout her career. Pattie also developed the PattieWack™ pompom and tassel making tools more than 15 years ago and is always eager to share her crafty ideas for using pompoms and tassels.

Recently, Pattie's passion for turning unconventional materials into fashion has elevated her craft to couture and put her in the runway spotlight at a fashion show called Trashique, which is held to raise funds for the Fresno Art Museum. Turning trash into fashion is now one of Pattie's favorite challenges. She's used recycled materials like VHS tapes to make giant pompoms for a 15-foot boa and dozens of used dryer sheets to make a giant hoopskirt.

Pattie is a design consultant for creative companies specializing in craft products, and she has traveled internationally to teach and inspire others to be makers and artists. With nearly 4 million views and 19 thousand followers on YouTube, Pattie has become an influencer on all social media platforms, creating crafty projects and costumes. Pattie can be seen on her website at ***www.pattiewack.com***, and on Etsy, Instagram, YouTube, Facebook, LinkedIn, and Pinterest as PattieWack Designs.

Pattie shares her entrepreneurial creative spirit with her husband, Scott Wilkinson, who is a corporate media manager specializing in video and photography. Together, they work in the craft industry to produce visual assets from their home studio in the California Central Valley. Pattie's family, including mom and dad, kids, and grandkids are spread out across Oklahoma and Mississippi. She sees them as often as she can and loves when they come to visit her, Scott, and their two dachshunds, Jens and Otto.

Pattie hopes her assemblage skills and knowledge of craft products, combined with her love of making something extraordinary from the ordinary, will ignite your creativity and build your confidence and sense of adventure. Have fun with it!

Contents

Meet the Author 02
Introduction to Cosplay 06
Getting Started 10
The Costumes 22
Unicorn Fairy. 24
Nordic Princess 34
Woodland Fox. 40
Lollipop Girl 48
American Superhero. 58
Centurion Gladiator 70
Top-Tier Ninja. 78
Sea God 88
Makeup 98
Patterns 100
Croquis Sketchbook 116

Introduction to Cosplay

Cosplay invites you into a realm where fantasy meets fashion. The term originated in Japan in 1984. It's a combination of the words costume and play, which defines dressing up and role-playing fictional characters from anime, manga, comic books, movies, books, video games, and television shows. Cosplay can mean the actual costume, as well as the action of wearing it, so it's both a noun and a verb. Cosplay is for everyone, from the beginner to the professional. It starts with an interest or even a passion for a fictional character and progresses to creating a costume that is worn for performing and pretending to be that character

Why is cosplay so popular? Maybe because every time we put on a costume, the player in us comes alive. Suddenly, a mask and a cape can turn anyone into a superhero, or a tutu and a horn can transform you into a unicorn!

Where do you cosplay? Cosplayers can find a plethora of places to wear their costumes at conventions, competitions, movie openings, live appearances, and charity events. Cosplay has become so popular that it encompasses all ages and has developed a global attraction for people around the world. More than 30 countries are represented at the annual World Cosplay Summit in Japan.

What are the different types of cosplay? In addition to traditional cosplay, where you mimic favorite characters, there are other forms of cosplay like crossplay and steampunk. Crossplay is dressing up as a character of the opposite gender. Steampunk is putting a twist on a character by recreating it with a Victorian aesthetic and replacing technological devices with gears and old-world assemblage. Then there are cosplay mash-ups, where you morph two or more characters together to create a one-of-a-kind costume for a unique cosplay experience.

Who are cosplayers? Some cosplay fans go to conventions as curious onlookers, while others have turned their passion into a business with photography, videos, and handmade costumes for sale. Sometimes people have the wrong idea about cosplay, like assuming that it's exclusive to geeky or nerdy people. You may think cosplayers are a hardcore community of over-obsessive nerds who have taken their love of science fiction or video gaming to a whole new level, and you are not invited.

On the contrary, the whole idea of cosplay is that it's for everyone, whether you make a costume from cardboard in an afternoon or you spend a month carving foam to create your perfect character. Depending on the character, some costumes can be alluring. While some cosplayers take advantage of this playful, sexy approach to the costumes, as a whole, the cosplay community is wholesome and family-friendly.

Are there cosplay rules? When it comes to creating a cosplay costume, the sky's the limit! But there are a few things to consider if you're getting more serious about cosplay. Be aware of copyright infringement and avoid branding yourself or your cosplay with a name that directly infringes on the original brand of your character. Simply give your costume a more generic name instead of a specific branded name. Also, be respectful when taking photos of fellow cosplayers and posting them on social media. Always ask permission before taking photos and sharing them on your social platforms. Chances are, most cosplayers will be happy to strike a pose!

Can I compete in cosplay? Cosplay competitions are perfect for crafters who take pride in the fabrication and intricate details of costuming and enjoy acting out their character on stage. Many cosplay conventions have competitions with prizes and awards. Sometimes, the judges are highly regarded celebrities in the cosplay realm, which adds to the thrill of the competition! There are all kinds of competitions and categories, so do some research to learn more and check out the rules before entering.

How do I get started with cosplay? Whether you're a beginner or you aspire to become a professional cosplayer, all you need is commitment and creativity. If you're reading this, then you've already committed to finding out what it takes to become a cosplayer. The next step is to let your creativity lead you in making a costume that you will find fun to wear, and you'll be transported into the fascinating realm of cosplay!

Getting Started

There are so many different ways to craft cosplay costumes. You can build on top of basic garments like hoodies or tank tops. You can sew your own garments. You can mold and shape foam into weapons or armor. You can glue pieces together and embellish them with duct tape or paint. In this section, you'll learn about gathering inspiration for a cosplay design and some of the different materials and tools you can use to bring it to life.

Using **Inspiration Boards**

When designing your own cosplay, try creating an inspiration board to conceptualize your costume. Inspiration boards, sometimes called mood boards or vision boards are my favorite tool for designing pretty much anything. As soon as I have an idea for something I want to create, I begin accumulating bits and pieces to pin to a board. Anything that inspires your design can be added, including fabric swatches, sketches, photos, magazine pages, words, quotes, objects, and samples of your test materials. You can even gather paint chips from the paint store to build a color palette. Gathering physical items can help you visualize your finished project and keep you on course as you make decisions throughout the design process.

Your board can be a poster, corkboard, a full wall, a notebook, or anything else that works for you. I love to use foam core board covered with fabric or felt, plus a handful of pins or tacks to use to attach items. Be sure your inspiration board is big enough to fit all of your materials and that it can be changed easily as your ideas evolve.

Of course, you can go digital with your inspiration boards—there are plenty of online sites where you can pin ideas and images. But physical objects trigger a different part of our brains than digital images, with textures and a tactile experience. So I encourage you to give a physical inspiration board a try. There's nothing like being able to touch and feel fuzzy faux fur, silky satin, seashells, or a fisherman's net.

I like to make a small board for each project I'm working on so I can grab it and take it with me as I work—to the sewing machine, the cutting table, or out in the garage where I work with foam. A portable board works well for me, but you might like one large board or wall where your entire process takes place. Do what works for you!

While the creative process continues, you may find it helpful to pin your croquis (fashion sketch) to your inspiration board, along with the measurements of the cosplayer you're designing for. Make a copy of the croquis or tear one of the croquis pages from this workbook to pin to your board.

Take a snapshot of your board with your phone and use the photo when shopping for supplies to be sure you're choosing materials in the right colors, sizes, and styles.

Whether you're designing for yourself or a high-profile client, the visuals on your inspiration board will help keep things crystal clear. Let your inspiration board motivate you and make it easy to create a cosplay experience you will love!

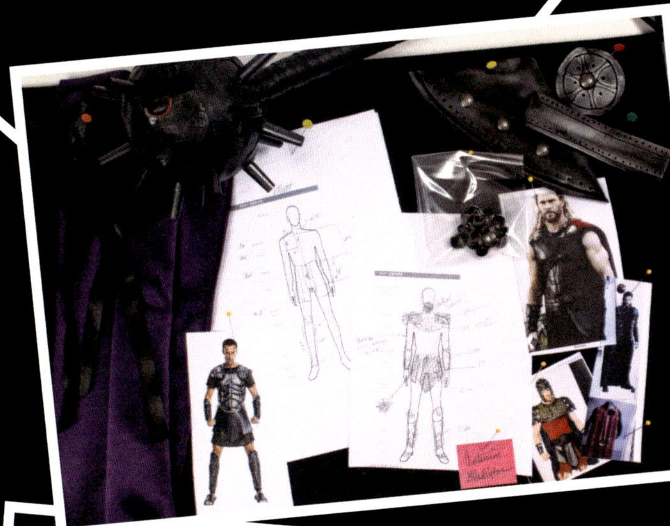

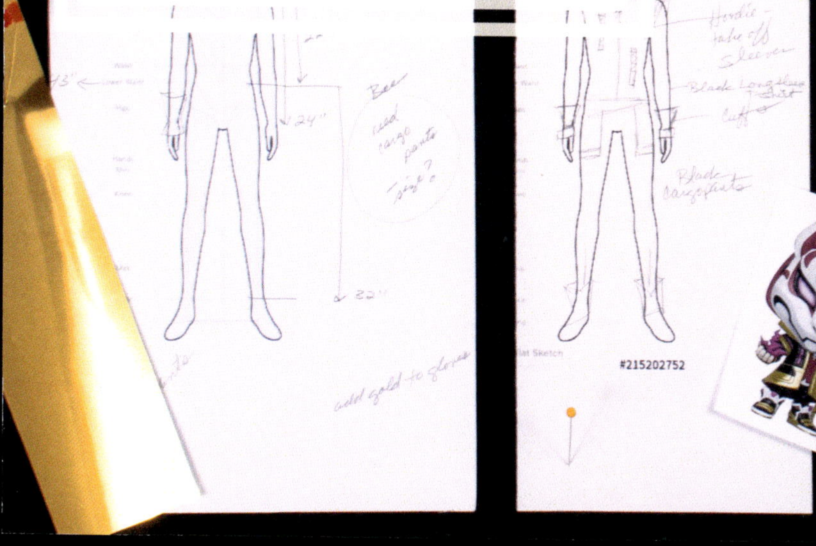

Choosing **Substrates**

Choosing substrates (the base garments) for your costume is the first step to making your cosplay work for you. Whether you build from a pair of leggings and a hoodie or a pile of fabric is totally up to you. Think about your sewing skills, how much time you want to spend, and what your budget is before you begin. The croquis pages in this workbook will help you get your plan in writing and create a visual of colors and shapes. It's amazing how helpful it is to know what you want and go from there. Here are some common substrates to consider.

Basic Garments

Simple garments like t-shirts, leggings, hoodies, and sweatpants are ideal for building a costume, especially for the beginner. These pieces come in every color imaginable and can be painted, embellished, and altered to make your design come to life. Sometimes you can find garments at thrift shops that only need a few alterations to transform them into the ultimate cosplay piece.

Fabric

Non-fraying fabrics are the best to use for cosplay substrates. These fabrics will not fray along the edges when cut, making them ideal for garments that are difficult to hem, like a circle skirt. When choosing fabrics for your costume, think about the fabric weight and the effect you're trying to create. Thin, see-through fabrics like webbing or tulle are great for light, fanciful pieces like a tutu or wings. Heavier satin fabrics that look beautiful when draped are perfect for capes. Faux fabrics are fun for creating realistic-looking leather or fur costume pieces. Metallic fabrics can enhance a costume with shiny effects.

Unconventional Materials

Unusual materials sometimes make perfect cosplay substrates. Quilted fabric pads used to protect furniture when moving are large and inexpensive. They're great for heavy items like coats and soft armor. The quilted fabric makes an impactful statement and can be painted, hemmed, surged, or edged with duct tape.

Thermal barrier fabric like OlyFun™ or Solarize can be used for beautiful accents, like in the Unicorn Fairy Tutu (page 28), where it's cut into strips and tied between layers of tulle. The material is stiff, but still flexible enough to manipulate. It comes in gold and silver, making it the perfect accent for a glitzy costume.

QUILTED FABRIC

THERMAL FABRIC

Foam

Foam comes in many forms and has many uses. This substrate is popular with cosplayers creating molded and sculpted costumes. When choosing foam, consider how thick, pliable, and heavy you'd like your finished piece to be. You'll also need to think about the tools you'll need to cut, sculpt, and attach the foam when building your costume. Keep any scraps leftover after cutting out your foam pieces. They can be used to experiment and test your design concept before you start on the garment itself.

Working with **Foam**

CRAFT FOAM

EVA FOAM

There are many ways to use foam for cosplay accessories and wearables. Using a heat gun, or even the heat of the sun, you can easily form the foam into the exact shape you need. Foam comes in different thicknesses so you can layer it without adding weight to your costume. Most foam is easy to cut with scissors or a utility knife, while more rigid foam can be sculpted with a heat tool and sanded to make smooth curves. Gluing can be done with a hot glue gun or contact cement. Foam can also be painted with acrylic paints and metallic waxes. After painting, you can cover the surface with a decoupage sealer to protect the finish.

When applying heat to foam with a heat gun, wear heat-proof gloves to prevent burns. You'll also need to wear a face mask that covers your nose and mouth and work in a well-ventilated area any time you're applying heat to foam. Children and pets should not be allowed to be in your foam workspace and kept away from all things that could harm them. Be responsible and be safe!

Craft Foam

Craft foam sheets can be found in most craft stores in a rainbow of colors. The sheets are 12" x 18" and 2 mm thick. This foam is great for creating layers and details on costumes like ears, horns, and raised decorative areas. Foam sheets can be cut with scissors or a craft knife. You can also use die-cutters to cut multiple identical pieces or more intricate designs.

EVA Foam

EVA is the acronym for ethylene-vinyl acetate. It's a high-density foam used for yoga mats, pipe insulation, sports gear, floor mats, and more. EVA foam has become a popular lightweight material for making the armor, swords, guns, shields, helmets, and other items that are vital for a cosplayer. Because EVA foam is a soft and sturdy material, it's easy to cut with basic tools like scissors or a box cutter. You can also use heat to mold, shape, and add texture to EVA foam. You can use plastic wrap to hold thin EVA foam against a form, then place it in the hot sun to set. EVA foam is available in craft stores in 24" x 40" black sheets in several thicknesses. You can also find it at hardware stores as ½"- and ¾"-thick flooring mat squares.

Household Foam

Household foam is 100% polyethylene and is sold as a utilitarian sheeting for insulation, to make a moisture barrier for camping, for yoga mats, and for padding sports equipment. Because it's so lightweight, household foam makes a great base for body armor. It can be molded with a heat gun like EVA foam and even embossed with a woodburning tool. It can also be painted and glued with hot glue. It's easy to cut with scissors or a utility knife. Household foam can be found in craft stores and online and is very affordable for large projects. The standard sizes for rolls are 72" x 24" x ¼" and 96" x 48" x ¼".

WORBLA

Worbla

Worbla is a brand of thermoplastic and very popular among serious cosplayers and prop artists. The material is mostly known for its use in shoemaking. Worbla has a natural adhesive that is activated when heated, allowing you to join two pieces together and to laminate layers easily. You can also use hot glue or an epoxy adhesive with Worbla. Worbla can be softened with heat and formed into any shape. When it's cold, it can be cut, carved, or sanded with woodworking hand tools. This foam should be stored somewhere that's between 30 and 120 degrees Fahrenheit. Be aware that if you leave Worbla in a hot car, it will soften and bond into one solid brick of plastic. Worbla can be purchased online and in some craft stores in 9.8" x 14.5" sheets in black and brown.

Working with **Adhesives**

Glue and tape are some of the best tools to use for making costumes. If the costume is never going to be thrown in a washing machine, you can use hot glue, tape, and craft glue to hold all the pieces together. Glue on embellishments, or even use tape, for a quick cosplay accent. Here are some gluing tips for no-sew costuming and embellishing.

Read and follow the manufacturer's instructions and always test the adhesive on a small piece of fabric or foam before starting your project. It's better to have a test piece fail than to glue an entire costume together only to have it fall apart during a fierce cosplay!

When working with adhesives, keep clothespins, masking tape, and straight pins handy to hold pieces together while the adhesive dries.

Some glues are very strong and should only be used in a well-ventilated area. This will be indicated on the label. When using strong glues like this, open your windows, turn on a fan, or work outside, especially if you're gluing foam pieces.

When working on intricate accents like a trim, use a piece of thick foam as your work surface. Once you glue the trim on, you can stick straight pins through the costume and into the foam to hold the trim in place while the glue dries. This is also a great way to add curves to trim.

Use non-stick scissors made especially for cutting tape and projects that have been glued. Keep the scissors clean and free from adhesive for a finer finish on projects.

Hot Glue

A hot glue gun and glue sticks are a way to assemble pieces almost instantly. Solid objects, as well as fabric, can be joined using hot glue. You can also use it to add embellishments to a finished piece. Keep a glass of water on hand when working with hot glue. If your fingers accidentally come in contact with the glue, dip them into the water so the glue cools immediately and peels off more easily.

FABRIC GLUE

Fabric Glue

Fabric glues come in squeeze bottles, tubes, and even sprays. Be sure to read the manufacturer's instructions before purchasing or using fabric glue. You'll want to be sure the glue you purchase works with the materials you have in mind. And you'll need to know if you should work in a well-ventilated area and how much time it will take the glue to set.

Duct Tape

Don't forget about tape! Duct tape is available in an array of colors and can be used to outline or accent a costume. Double-sided tape, such as red liner wig tape can be used to attach non-washable items.

Spray Adhesives

Spray adhesives are great for joining large pieces together. When using spray adhesives, be sure to work in a well-ventilated area and cover your work surface. There are spray adhesives made specifically for fabric, but if you don't intend to wash your costume, you can use any permanent spray adhesive. Spray adhesives have varying open and drying times and different methods for application. Be sure to read and follow the manufacturer's instructions for the best results.

DUCT TAPE

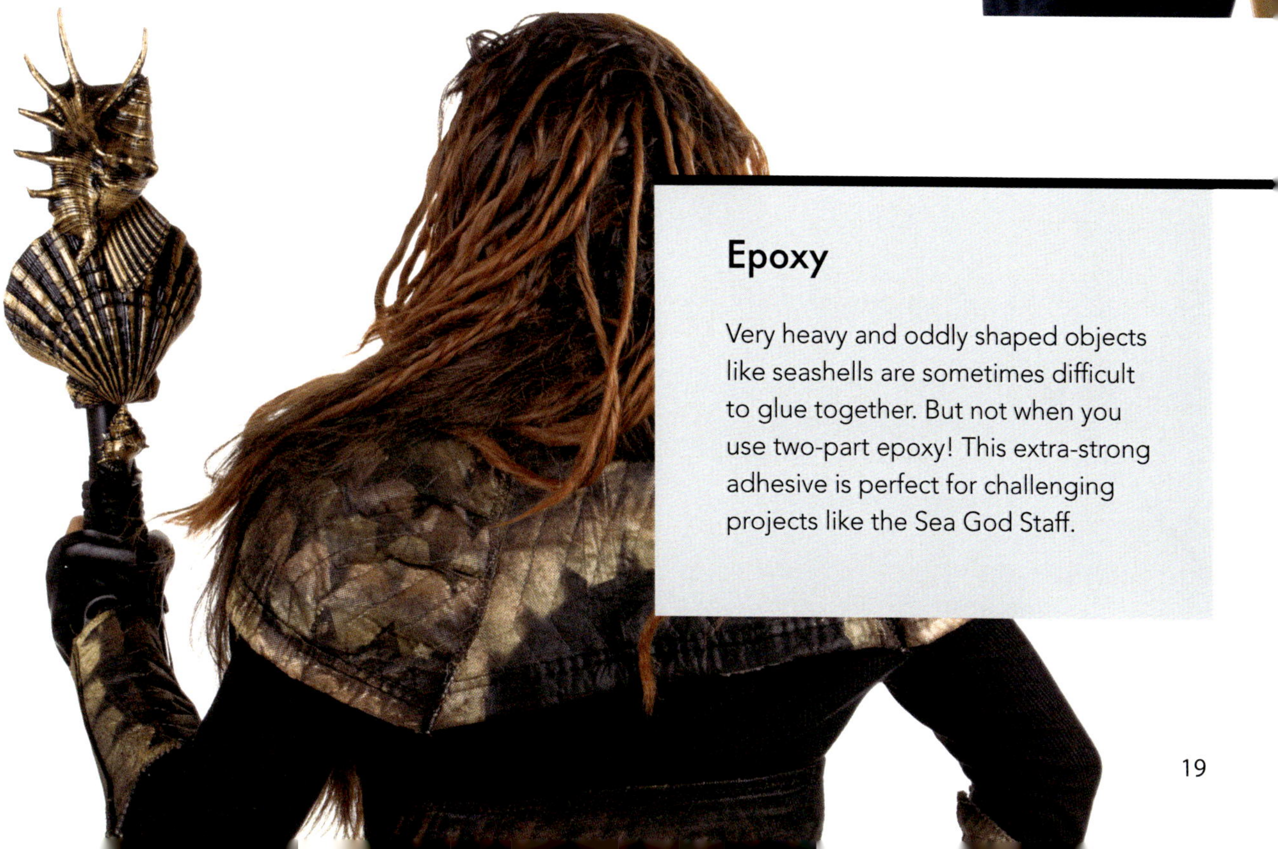

Epoxy

Very heavy and oddly shaped objects like seashells are sometimes difficult to glue together. But not when you use two-part epoxy! This extra-strong adhesive is perfect for challenging projects like the Sea God Staff.

Tools

The tools you use are very important when you value the outcome of a cosplay creation. Think about how the adventure began—with your vision of an amazing costume and walking into a room with all eyes on you. To make that adventure enjoyable, your tools should be an extension of your creativity.

Many makers, including me, have tools that have been inherited from a family member, like sewing machines and hand tools. Keep them in good shape and learn the value of having the right tool for the job. Treat your tools with respect, and you will soon have a favorite, whether it's a vintage sewing machine, a great soldering iron, or maybe a brand-new 3D printer. Here are a few of my favorite tools for cosplay creating.

CUTTING TOOLS

Power Tools

- Cordless drill
- Hot glue gun
- Heat gun
- Woodburning tool
- Steam iron

Hand Tools & Protective Gear

- Hammer
- Pliers
- Clamps
- Gloves
- Mask
- Leather punch
- Blunt-nose scissors

Craft Tools

- Disposable plates and cups
- Cotton swabs
- Clothespins
- Binder clips
- Sponge
- Pins
- Craft knives
- Paintbrushes
- Zip ties
- Chopsticks
- Permanent marker
- Pencil
- Disposable gloves

Cutting Tools

- Self-healing cutting mat
- Cutting ruler
- Metal ruler
- Measuring tape
- Rotary cutting tools
- Scissors
- Tailor's chalk

The Costumes

Enter the realm of cosplay and amaze your friends and family with your superhero crafting skills. This cosplay workbook is designed to be your resource for low-sew and no-sew costume making. Inside, you'll find step-by-step instructions and super-simple patterns for cosplay pieces that you can mix and match and customize to create so many different costumes!

You'll find 8 inspiration costumes in this workbook. You can recreate them exactly or customize the pieces to design your own unique characters! Use the Croquis Sketchbook pages to jot down measurements and sketch ideas, then bring your designs to life!

Unicorn Fairy

Nordic Princess

Woodland Fox

Lollipop Girl

American Superhero

Centurion Gladiator

Top-Tier Ninja

Sea God

Unicorn Fairy

Unicorn Fairy Costume Pieces

Headdress.................... 26
Tutu.......................... 28
Wings........................ 30
Headband.................... 32
Tank Top Dress............... 33
Leg Wraps.................... 92
Fingerless Gloves 80

All it takes is your imagination and tons of tulle to make this Unicorn Fairy come alive. The headdress is a simple faux fur hat with a tulle mane, plus a headband with ears and a golden horn with beaded accents. The wings are made from wire and sheer fusible web edged with glass beads, plus ribbons to attach them. Lace is used to enhance a tank top dress, which is worn with a tulle tutu over white tights. Furry fingerless gloves and leg wraps complete the look. You'll be flying high in the sky when you show up at the next convention as a Unicorn Fairy!

Unicorn Fairy **Headdress**

Shopping List

- ¼ yd white faux fur
- White thread
- ¼ yd each of 54"-wide tulle in pink, white, turquoise, and lavender
- 2 yd white satin ribbon

Tools

- Pins
- Scissors
- Hot glue gun and glue sticks
- Ruler
- Rotary cutter
- Self-healing cutting mat

At first glance, this headdress may seem very complicated, but you'll find it's easy to make! It's simply a piece of faux fur sewn into a hood with a mane made of tulle and ribbon hot glued on top. Ribbon ties are used to hold the headdress in place under the cosplayer's chin. This pattern can be used for any furry creature. Simply change the color of the fur and tulle to match the character you're creating.

1. **Sew the headdress.** Make two copies of the headdress pattern on page 100. Pin the copies to the wrong side of the faux fur and cut them out. Following the letters on the pattern, pin and sew A to A with wrong sides facing to create pleats for the ears. Place the two pieces with right sides facing, matching up the carrot (<) symbols marked on the pattern. Pin and sew the two pieces together along the curved edge.

2. **Add the ties.** Cut two 18"-long pieces of ribbon. Sew a ribbon to each corner of the headdress at the Xs marked on the pattern to create ties.

3. **Make the mane.** Cut the tulle into 6" x 12" strips, cutting 25 strips of each color. Cut a 24"-long piece of ribbon. Tie the tulle strips to the ribbon to create the mane.

4. **Attach the mane.** Turn the headdress right side out. Hot glue the mane over the center seam of the headdress from the crown to the nape. The mane is longer than the headdress, so the end should hang down from the back of the headdress.

Unicorn Fairy **Tutu**

Shopping List

- 3 yd ribbon
- 5 yd of 54"-wide tulle in beige
- 6 yd of 54"-wide tulle in white
- 1½ yd each of 54"-wide tulle in lavender, pink, and turquoise
- Silver OlyFun™ fabric

Tools

- Tape measure
- Rotary cutter
- Self-healing cutting mat
- Ruler

1. **Tie the ribbon.** Measure the cosplayer's waist to determine the size of the tutu. Tie two knots in the ribbon, making the space between them the same measurement as the cosplayer's waist.

2. **Cut the tulle.** Use a rotary cutter and self-healing cutting mat to cut the tulle into 6" x 27" strips. You'll need 18 strips each of the lavender, pink, and turquoise, 72 strips of white, and 60 strips of beige.

3. **Tie the tulle.** Tie the tulle strips to the ribbon between the two knots. As you add strips, push them close together so the ribbon is completely covered between the two knots.

4. **Add the OlyFun™.** For extra flair, cut the OlyFun™ into 18 strips that are 6" x 27" and tie them onto the ribbon, distributing them evenly throughout the tulle.

Unicorn Fairy **Wings**

Shopping List

- 2 wire clothes hangers
- White felt
- Double-sided fusible webbing (I used Stick™ Double-Sided Fusible Web by Fairfield™)
- 2 single light switch covers with screws and bolts
- White zip ties
- Glass microbeads
- 2"-wide white satin ribbon

Tools

- Spray adhesive
- Hot glue gun and glue sticks
- Scissors
- Wire cutters

1. **Shape the wings.** Follow the wings pattern on page 101 to form both wire hangers into the wing shape. Use zip ties to hold the ends of the wire together.

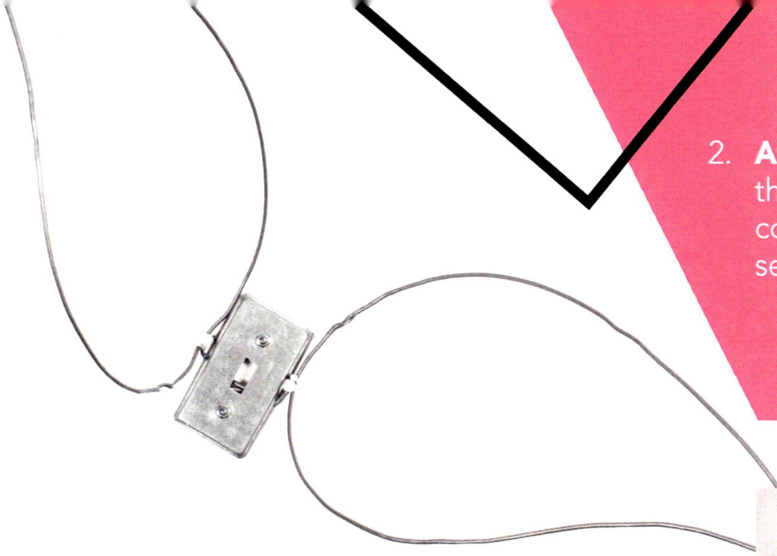

2. **Attach the wings.** Place the ends of the wings between the two light switch covers and screw the covers together, securing them with the bolts.

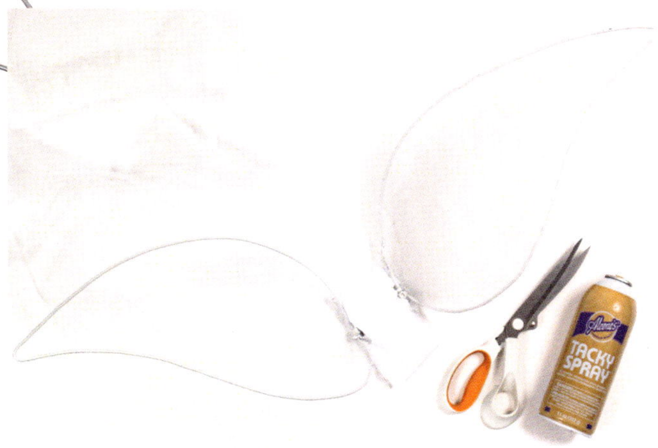

3. **Add the felt.** Use glue and felt to cover the light switch covers and protect the cosplayer from any sharp points when wearing the wings.

4. **Attach the webbing.** Cut 4 pieces of webbing that are 2" larger on all sides than the wings. Working on a covered work surface, spray one side of a wing with spray adhesive and press a piece of webbing onto it with your fingers. Turn the wing over, spray adhesive onto the other side, and press another piece of webbing onto it with your fingers. Trim away the excess webbing around the edge of the wing with non-stick scissors. Repeat for the other wing.

5. **Add the beads.** Spray adhesive around the edges of the wings and pour glass microbeads onto the wet adhesive. Repeat as needed to get heavy coverage with the beads around the edges. Let dry.

6. **Add the ties.** Tie the ribbon around the center of the wings. Use the ends of the ribbon to tie the wings to the cosplayer. Loop the ribbon ends over the cosplayer's shoulders from back to front. Then bring the ends under the cosplayer's arms and around the back and tie them in a bow at the center of the wings.

Unicorn Fairy **Headband**

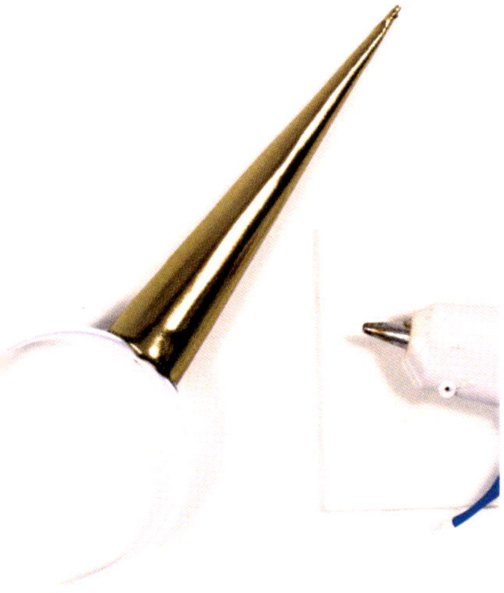

Shopping List

- White headband
- Heavy cardstock
- Metallic fabric
- White faux fur
- Gray felt
- Silver embroidered collar
- Beaded necklace

Tools

- Hot glue gun and glue sticks
- Scissors

1. **Make the horn.** Use the heavy cardstock to form a 9"-tall cone for the horn. Cover the horn with metallic fabric and glue it to the center of the headband.

2. **Make the ears.** Using the pattern on page 102, cut two ears from the felt and two ears from the faux fur. Hot glue the felt ears to the wrong side of the fur ears. Pinch the base of each ear together and hot glue in place. Then hot glue the ears to the headband on either side of the horn.

3. **Embellish.** Hot glue the silver embroidered collar to the front of the headband. Wind the beaded necklace around the horn and glue into place.

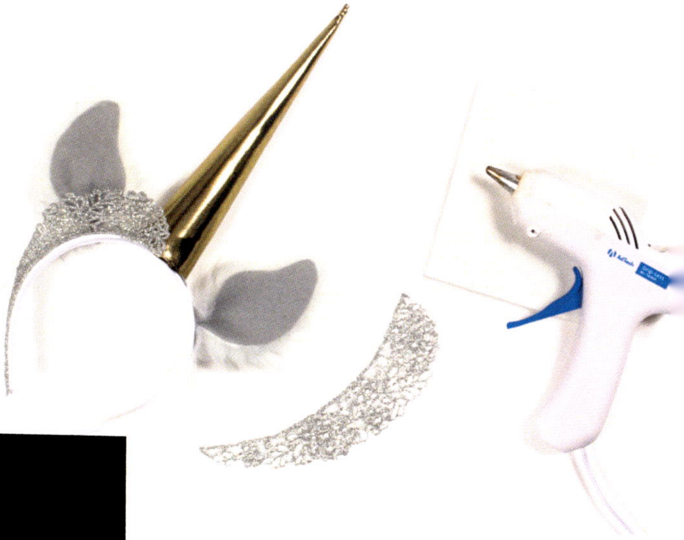

Unicorn Fairy Tank Top Dress

Shopping List

- White tank top dress
- Lace applique in silver and white
- Beaded necklace

Tools

- Fabric glue

1. **Embellish the dress.** Use fabric glue to layer and attach the lace applique to the front of the tank top dress. Glue the beaded necklace along the neckline.

Nordic Princess

Bring out your inner iron maiden with this fierce costume. This cosplay ensemble starts with your own gold bandeau worn underneath a belted black tunic. A red satin cape draped from the back and attached to the front at the shoulders indicates your royal status. The brown faux leather armbands have furry strips at the top to form cuffs, with matching leg wraps and a capelet. The finishing touch is a dagger and a golden shield made of foam to stop any enemies in their tracks!

Nordic Princess Costume Pieces

Capelet 36
Cape.......... 60
Armbands.......... 92
Leg Wraps.......... 92
Shield & Dagger 38

Nordic Princess **Capelet**

Shopping List

- ⅓ yd faux fur
- 1 yd of ½"-wide ribbon or faux leather

Tools

- Tape measure
- Scissors
- Hot glue gun and glue sticks

A capelet is a mini cape that lies across the cosplayer's shoulders and has ribbon or faux leather ties. You can make multiple capelets in different colors of faux fur and varying lengths to wear in layers and create a very dramatic look for a wintery costume.

1. **Cut the fabric.** Measure and cut the faux fur to the size you need for your capelet using the diagram on page 103 for reference. For the length, measure the cosplayer from shoulder to shoulder and add 12". For the width, measure 12".

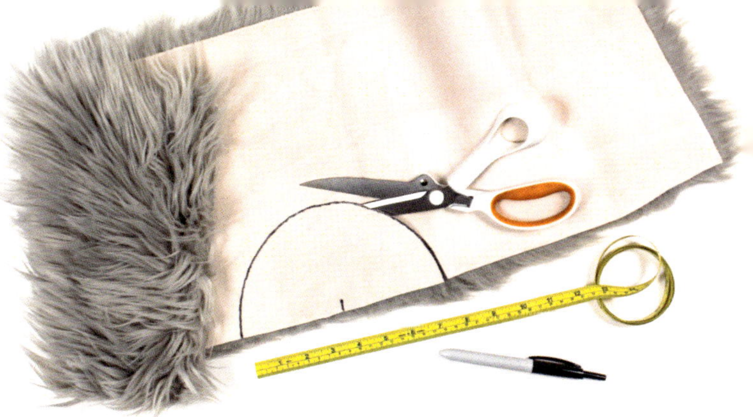

2. **Cut the neck.** In the center of one long side, cut out an 8"-diameter half-circle using the diagram on page 103 for reference.

3. **Trim the corners.** Round off all of the corners.

4. **Finish the edges.** Along all the sides, turn the fur under and hot glue it to the back of the fabric.

5. **Add the ties.** Cut the ribbon or faux leather in half so you have two equally sized pieces. Hot glue one piece on each side of the half-circle at the Xs marked on the pattern to create ties.

Nordic Princess
Shield & Dagger

Shopping List
- Worbla foam sheet
- Plastic domed trashcan lid
- Cardboard
- Leather lacing
- Rub n' Buff® in silver and gold
- Metal drawer pull
- Large gold button

Tools
- Woodburning tool
- Plastic wrap
- Packing tape
- Scissors
- Tailor's chalk
- Hot glue gun and glue sticks

1. **Make the shield.** Follow the instructions on page 68 to make a shield. Use a pointed woodburning tool to emboss a sunburst pattern on the front as shown. Apply gold Rub n' Buff®, highlighting the embossed sections of the design. Let dry, then add additional highlights to emphasize the design. Glue a large gold button in the center.

2. **Make the dagger.** Cut pieces for the dagger hilt and blade from cardboard and glue them together. Let dry, then apply silver Rub n' Buff® to the finished dagger blade and hilt. Apply several coats, rubbing the dagger with a soft cloth between coats to create a fine metal-like finish. Wrap leather lacing around the handle.

Woodland Fox

Woodland Fox Costume Pieces

Tail. 42
Waist Cincher 44
Headband. 46
Circle Skirt 50
Fingerless Gloves 80

Be prepared to cuddle up in this cute little woodland costume made with fuzzy faux fur fabrics. The faux fur ears on the headband match the faux fur that's glued to the bust of a brown tank top. The waist cincher has grommets with leather lacing. A circle skirt edged with fur trim coordinates with fur-edged fingerless gloves. Furry strips wrapped around the boots and a big fat fuzzy tail will have you handing out sassy hugs at the next convention!

Woodland **Fox Tail**

Shopping List
- ¼ yd faux fur
- Matching thread
- D-ring
- Fiberfill stuffing

Tools
- Tape measure
- Scissors
- Pins
- Hot glue gun and glue sticks

Every fox needs a tail, and some foxes need ***nine*** tails! But not only foxes—there are so many furry cosplay characters who need tails, you're sure to use this pattern over and over again to complete your costumes. You can customize this design by making it shorter or longer, wider or narrower, or from a different fabric to create the perfect tail for your cosplay!

1. **Cut the fabric.** Measure the tail pattern on page 104 and adjust the size as needed. Use the pattern to cut two tail pieces from the faux fur.

2. **Sew the tail.** Pin the two pieces together with right sides facing and sew around the edges, leaving a 4" opening for turning.

3. **Stuff.** Turn the tail right side out and fill with stuffing. Hot glue the opening closed.

4. **Finish.** Thread the top of the tail through a D-ring, fold over, and hot glue in place. Use the D-ring to attach the tail to your costume.

Woodland Fox **Waist Cincher**

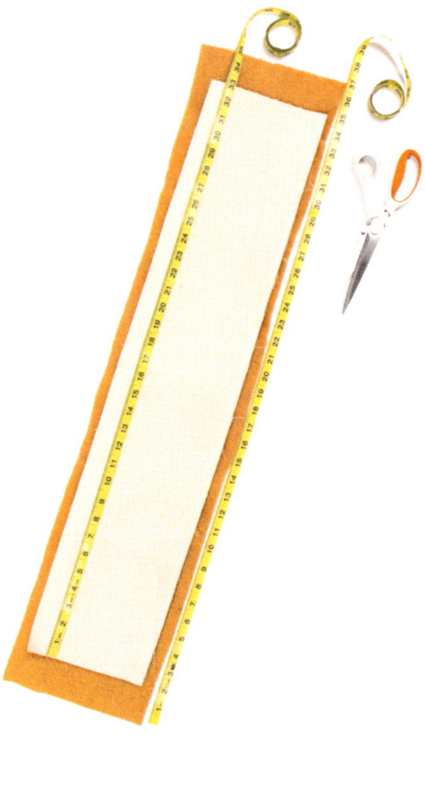

Shopping List

- ¼ yd tan felt
- ¼ yd heavy canvas fabric
- Matching thread
- Grommets
- Leather lace

Tools

- Tape measure
- Scissors
- Pins
- Hot glue gun and glue sticks

1. **Cut the fabric.** Measure the cosplayer's waist. Cut a piece of canvas to the same length as the cosplayer's waist measurement and to the width you'd like the waist cincher to be. Cut a piece of felt 4" longer and 2" wider than the canvas.

2. **Finish the edges.** With right sides facing down, center the piece of canvas on top of the felt. Fold the felt over the edges of the canvas and sew or hot glue into place.

3. **Attach the grommets.** Following the manufacturer's instructions, attach grommets to both ends of the waist cincher.

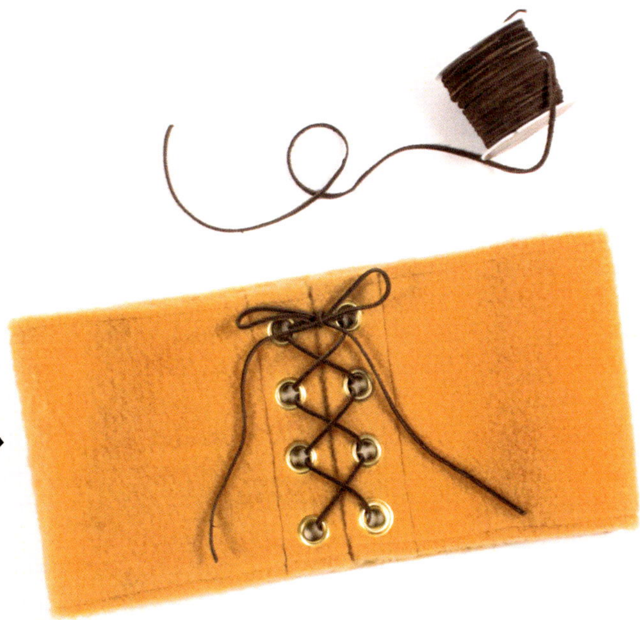

4. **Make the closure.** Weave the leather lace through the grommets in a crisscross pattern to form a closure.

Woodland Fox **Headband**

Shopping List
- Brown headband
- Brown faux fur
- Tan felt

Tools
- Tape measure
- Scissors
- Hot glue gun and glue sticks

1. **Cut the fabric.** Cut two 5" x 5" squares from the felt and two 5" x 5" squares from the faux fur.

2. **Make the ears.** Hot glue the felt squares to the wrong sides of the fur squares. Wrap the squares around the headband to form triangles as shown and hot glue in place.

3. **Trim.** Trim away any excess fabric as close to the headband as possible to complete the ears.

Lollipop Girl

Lollipop Girl Costume Pieces

Circle Skirt 50

Hoodie 54

Leggings & Boots 55

Cap & Backpack 57

Sweeten up your cosplay game with this yummy candy-accented costume. The cap, hoodie, backpack, and circle skirt all have real candy pieces glued to them to enhance the whimsical look. The leggings have been painted with white stripes, and the boots are accented with bright pink spray paint and a single candy glued to the toes. Fill your backpack with candy when you head out to your next video game event, and you'll get tons of "likes" from fans who love their sweets!

Lollipop Girl **Circle Skirt**

Use these instructions to create the circle skirt for the Woodland Fox using brown felt and faux fur trim.

Shopping List

- 1¼ yd fuchsia felt
- Matching thread
- One 3"-long piece of sew-on hook-and-loop tape
- Fuchsia fabric spray paint
- Candy pieces

Tools

- Tape measure
- Scissors
- Permanent marker
- Pins
- Masking tape
- Hot glue gun and glue sticks

This circle skirt may look complicated, but it's one of the simplest skirts to make and can be used in lots of cosplay! Measuring is super easy—you just need to know the waist measurement of the cosplayer and length you want the skirt to be. This piece works best with non-fraying fabrics like felt, which was used for both the Woodland Fox and the Lollipop Girl. Heavy fabrics are good for this skirt because they give it volume. Consider adding a cancan underskirt for a super flirty look.

Waist Measurement Chart

Waist Measurement	Waist Radius
23"	3⅜"
24"	3½"
25"	3⅝"
26"	3⅞"
27"	4"
28"	4¼"
29"	4½"
30"	4½"
31"	4¾"
32"	5"
33"	5"
34"	5¼"
35"	5½"
36"	5½"
37"	5¾"
38"	5⅞"
39"	6"
40"	6¼"
41"	6½"
42"	6½"
43"	6¾"
44"	6¾"
45"	7"

1. **Cut the fabric.** Use the chart to determine the cosplayer's waist radius measurement. Add the waist radius to the length you want the skirt to be plus 1". This is the full skirt radius. (Use the diagram on page 105 for reference.) Fold the fabric in half from corner to corner. Fold again from corner to corner. Pin a measuring tape to the center point at the measurement for the full skirt radius. Use the end of the tape measure and a permanent marker to mark the full skirt radius measurement on the fabric. Cut through all the layers of fabric along the mark.

2. **Cut the waist.** Re-pin the measuring tape to the center point at the measurement for the waist radius. Use the end of the tape and a permanent marker to mark the waist radius measurement on the fabric. Cut through all the layers of fabric along the mark.

3. **Cut the closure.** From the waist opening, cut a 3" to 4" slit to create a closure for the skirt..

4. **Cut the waistband.** Cut a piece of felt 4" wide and the length of the cosplayer's full waist measurement plus 3". This will be the waistband of the skirt.

5. **Attach the waistband.** Pin the waistband around the waist opening of the skirt with right sides together, leaving a 3" tab at one end. Sew the waistband to the skirt.

6. **Sew the ends.** Turn the waistband up, then fold it in half with right sides together. Fold and pin the short end as shown in the photo, then sew it in place. Pin and sew around the open edges of the tab.

7. **Finish the waistband.** Trim off the corners, then turn the waistband right side out. Turn under the edge and pin it in place. Topstitch along the open edge to finish.

8. **Finish the closure.** Sew the pieces of hook-and-loop tape to the waistband on each side of the slit to finish the closure.

9. **Mark the pleat pattern.** Place the skirt on a covered work surface. Apply masking tape to the right side of the skirt as shown to cover the areas you don't want to paint.

10. **Paint the skirt.** Working in a well-ventilated area, spray fuchsia spray paint over the entire skirt. Let the paint dry, then remove all the masking tape.

11. **Attach candy.** Glue candy pieces around the edge of the skirt.

Lollipop Girl **Hoodie**

Shopping List

- Fuchsia hoodie
- Green fabric paint
- Cardboard t-shirt form
- Candy pieces

Tools

- Masking tape
- Pins
- Foam brush
- Hot glue gun and glue sticks
- Scissors

1. **Secure the hoodie.** Place the cardboard t-shirt form inside the hoodie. Pin the hoodie in place at the back of the t-shirt form so the front of the hoodie is flat for painting.

2. **Paint.** Apply masking tape to the front of the hoodie to create a V shape. Paint the V green and let it dry.

3. **Cut the shoulders.** To create a peek-a-boo opening for the shoulders, cut a 6" slit along the shoulder seam at the top of the sleeve. Then cut back across the sleeve. Leave the edges of the opening raw or finish them with a ¼" hem.

4. **Attach the candy.** Glue candy pieces on top of the green stripe.

Lollipop Girl
Leggings & Boots

Shopping List
- Black leggings
- Ankle boots
- Fabric spray paint in white and fuchsia
- Candy pieces

Tools
- Masking tape
- Hot glue gun and glue sticks

1. **Mark the stripe pattern.** Place the leggings on a covered work surface. Apply masking tape to the front of the leggings in a stripe pattern as shown to cover the areas you don't want to paint.

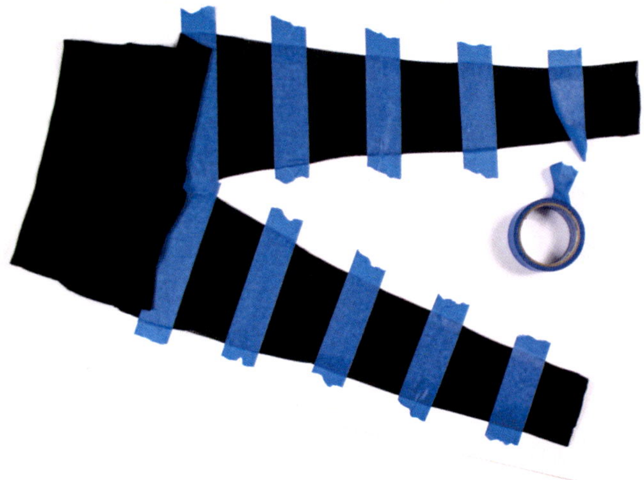

2. **Paint the leggings.** Working in a well-ventilated area, spray white spray paint over the leggings and let them dry. Remove the masking tape. Turn the leggings over and repeat Steps 1–2 on the back, matching the stripes.

3. **Cover the boots.** Place the boots on a covered work surface. Apply masking tape to the back half of each boot and the heels.

4. **Paint the boots.** Working in a well-ventilated area, spray fuchsia spray paint over the boots and let them dry. Remove the masking tape. Glue a piece of candy to the top of each boot.

Lollipop Girl **Cap & Backpack**

Shopping List

- Fuchsia ball cap
- Mini backpack
- Candy pieces

Tools

- Hot glue gun and glue sticks

1. **Embellish the cap.** Glue candy pieces across the front of the hat.
2. **Embellish the backpack.** Glue candy pieces to the front and around the edges of the backpack

American Superhero

American Superhero Costume Pieces

Cape 60
Masked Cap 62
Waist Cincher 66
Armbands 92
Leg Wraps 92
Shield 68

Save the day when you cosplay in this superhero outfit. You can hide behind the masked cap as you glide through comic-con wearing a floor-length red and blue satin cape. A blue sweatshirt with an iron-on star paired with dark blue jeans and brown leather boots are the basic garments, plus faux leather armbands, leg wraps, and a waist cincher. A foam shield is at the ready to ward off incoming destruction as this American hero fights against injustice!

American Superhero **Cape**

Use these instructions to create the cape for the Nordic Princess. Make the cape wider so it can come under the cosplayer's arms from the back and attach to the shoulders at the front.

Shopping List

- 1½ yd blue satin (cape front)
- 1½ yd red satin (cape back)
- Two 4"-long pieces of sew-on hook-and-loop tape
- Matching thread

Tools

- Measuring tape
- Scissors
- Pins

Use these instructions to create the cape for the Centurion Gladiator. Make the cape shorter and narrower and attach it to one shoulder.

Every superhero needs a cape to glide across cities, shield them from harm, and disorient their enemies. Other characters, like our Centurion Gladiator and Nordic Princess, wear them as a symbol of royalty or status. Use the measurements on your croquis and the cape pattern to determine the specific dimensions for your cosplayer. The instructions here are for the American Superhero cape. You can make the cape wider for a dramatically draped cape like the one the Nordic Princess wears or make it shorter and skinnier to attach it to one shoulder like the Centurion Gladiator's cape.

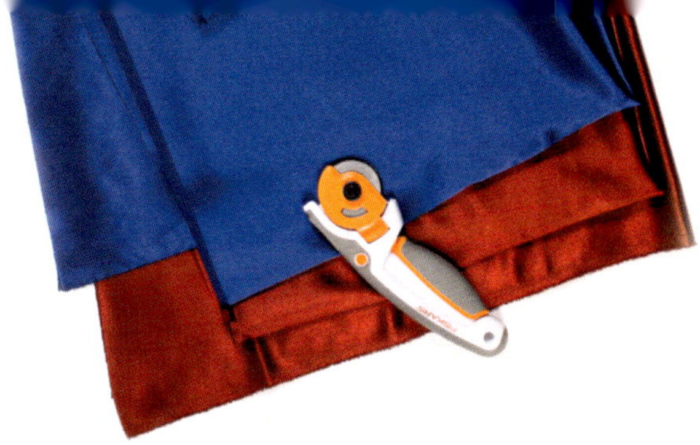

1. **Cut the fabric.** Measure and cut the fabric for the front and back of the cape to size using the diagram on page 106 for reference. For the length, measure from the cosplayer's shoulder to the floor. For the width, measure 36".

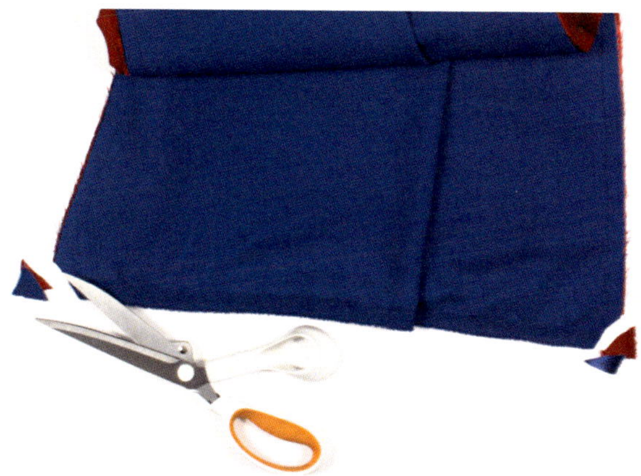

2. **Sew the cape.** Pin the fabric for the front and back of the cape together with right sides facing. Sew the pieces together along three sides using a ⅝" seam. Leave one of the short sides open.

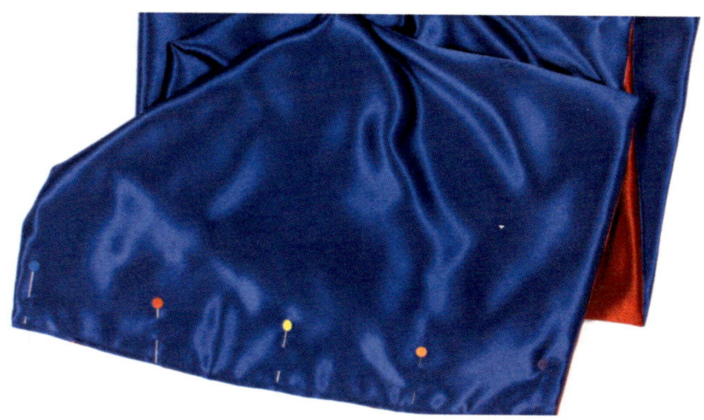

3. **Turn.** Trim the corners and turn the fabric right side out through the opening you left
in Step 2.

4. **Close the opening.** Turn the raw edges of the open side under and pin in place. Topstitch the opening closed to finish the cape.

5. **Attach the hook-and-loop tape.** Sew the hook pieces of the hook-and-loop tape to the back of the cape in the top corners. Sew the loop pieces of hook-and-loop tape to the shoulders of the superhero undergarment.

American Superhero **Masked Cap**

Shopping List

- ⅓ yd blue flannel
- Matching thread

Tools

- Chopstick or dowel rod
- Tape measure
- Scissors
- Pins
- Tailor's chalk

Some superheroes wear a mask to protect their identity so they can live a normal life when they've finished saving the world. For the American Superhero, this masked cap is made from blue flannel and can be adjusted in size to fit you perfectly. You can also use this pattern to make a simple beanie cap without the mask for everyday wear!

Cut out the cap. The pattern on page 107 is for a cap 21" around. Measure around the cosplayer's head and add 1" for the seam. Increase or decrease the size of the pattern to match the measurement. Make a copy of the cap pattern and pin it on top of two layers of the flannel. Cut out the pattern. One piece will be the outside of the cap and one piece will be the lining.

Sew the cap. Take the fabric for the outside of the cap and, with right sides facing, pin and sew the seams. Following the numbers on the pattern, pin and sew 1 to 1, 2 to 2, 3 to 3, and 4 to 4. Then pin and sew 5 to 5 and 6 to 6.

Attach the lining. Repeat Step 2 with the fabric for the lining of the cap. Place the lining inside the cap with right sides facing. Pin the lining and the outside of the cap together and sew, leaving a 4" opening for turning.

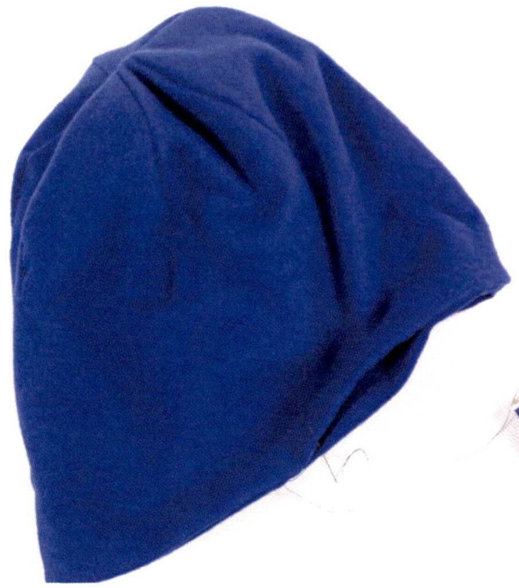

4. **Finish.** Turn the cap right side out and stitch the opening closed to finish.

5. **Cut out the mask.** Copy the mask pattern on page 108 and pin it on top of two layers of the flannel. Cut out the pattern, except for the eye openings. These will be cut out in a later step.

6. **Sew the mask.** With right sides facing, pin the two pieces of fabric for the mask together and sew, leaving a 2" opening for turning.

7. **Finish the edges.** Turn the mask right side out, using a dowel rod or chopstick to turn the smaller areas. Stitch the opening closed. Press the mask with an iron if needed.

8. **Mark the eye openings.** Use the copy of the mask pattern to check the position of the eye openings against your cosplayer. Enlarge or move the openings as needed to fit, then cut them out of the pattern. Lay the pattern on top of the mask and mark the eye openings with chalk.

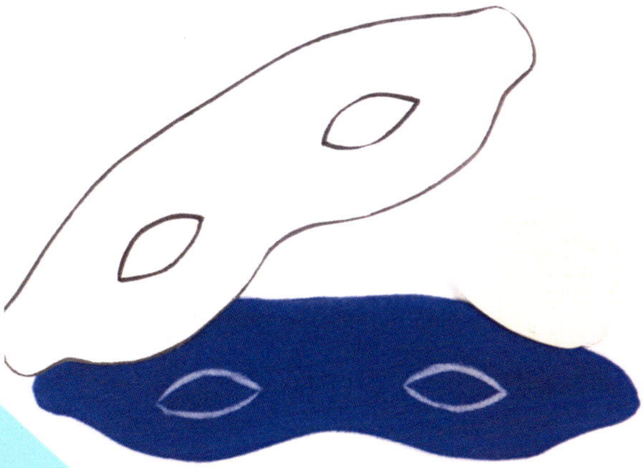

9. **Finish the eye openings.** Sew a zigzag or buttonhole stitch along the marks for the eye openings. Then cut out the eye openings, being careful not to cut the stitches.

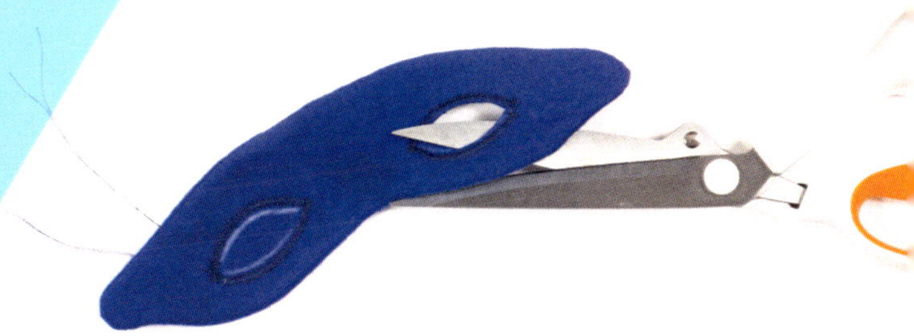

10. **Finish.** Pin and sew the mask to the front edge of the cap.

American Superhero Waist Cincher

Use these instructions to create the waist cincher for the Sea God using quilted fabric. Add a belt with a seashell and a fisherman's net.

Shopping List

- ½ yd white faux leather
- ½ yd heavy canvas fabric
- Matching thread
- White sew-on hook-and-loop tape
- Acrylic paint in red and burgundy

Tools

- Masking tape
- Tape measure
- Scissors
- Ruler
- Pencil
- Paintbrush

1. **Cut the fabric.** Measure the cosplayer's waist. Cut a piece of canvas to the same length as the cosplayer's waist measurement plus 6" and the width you'd like the waist cincher to be. Cut a piece of faux leather 4" longer and 2" wider than the canvas. Fold the edges of the faux leather over onto the canvas and sew them into place. Sew hook-and-loop tape to each end of the waist cincher for a closure.

2. **Paint the design.** Using a ruler and a pencil, mark your design on the faux leather. Apply the masking tape to block off areas of the design as needed. Mix the two red paint colors together and apply it to the faux leather with a medium-sized paintbrush. Let the paint dry, then peel away any masking tape you applied.

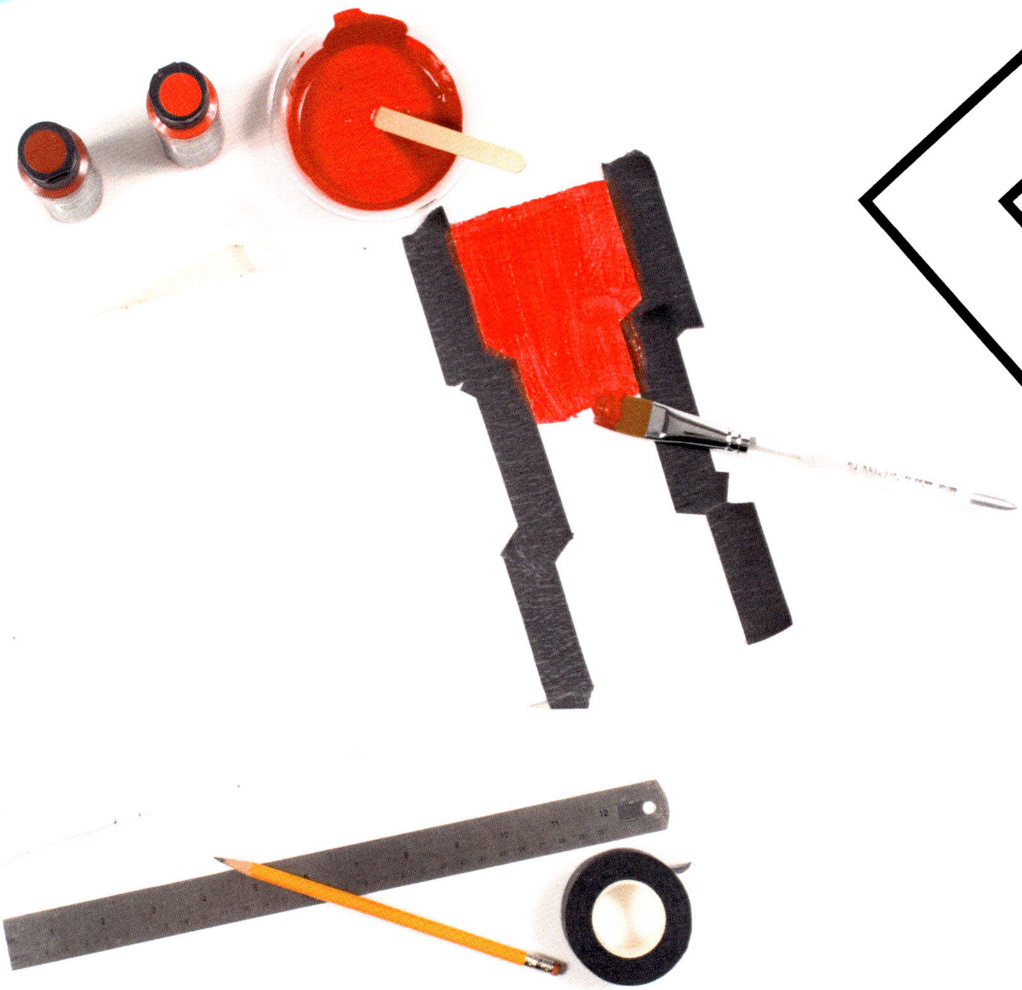

American Superhero **Shield**

Use these instructions to create the shield for the Nordic Princess.

Shopping List
- Medium-weight EVA foam sheet
- White craft foam
- Acrylic paint in red and blue
- Metal drawer pull
- Plastic domed trashcan lid

Tools
- Plastic wrap
- Packing tape
- Tailor's chalk
- Scissors
- Paintbrush
- Hot glue gun and glue sticks

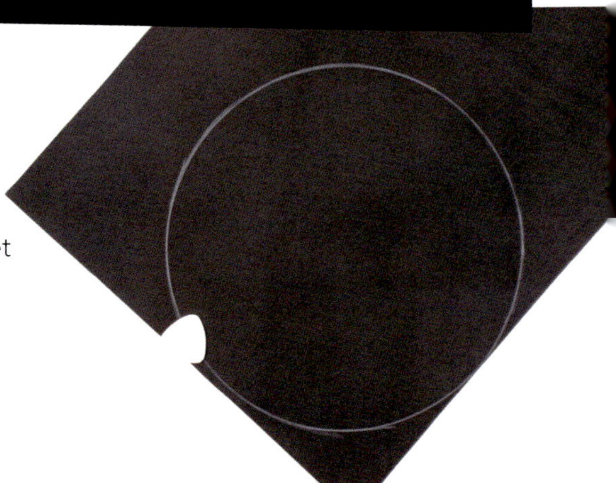

1. **Cut the foam.** Draw a circle the size you want the finished shield to be on EVA foam with chalk and cut it out.

2. **Shape the foam.** Place the foam circle on top of the domed trashcan lid and cover it completely with plastic wrap. Use packing tape to secure plastic wrap over the foam. Place the lid and foam outside in direct sunlight all day (8 hours).

3. **Paint.** Remove the foam from the trashcan lid. It should now have the same domed shape as the lid. Paint the outer rim of the shield red and let it dry. Paint the inside of the shield blue and let it dry.

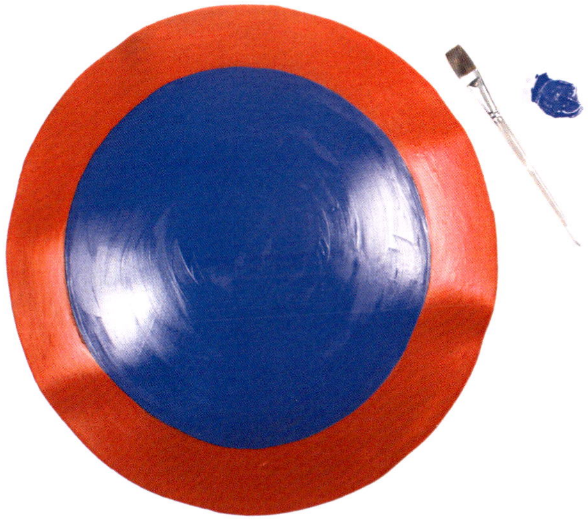

4. **Attach the star.** Using the pattern on page 109, cut the 5-point star from white foam and hot glue it to the center of the shield.

5. **Attach the handle.** Hot glue the metal drawer pull to the center of the back of the shield.

Centurion Gladiator

Get ready to do battle as a centurion gladiator, complete with shoulder pauldrons, kilt, arm guards, leg guards, and armor, all made from foam. The undergarments are a black long-sleeve shirt, a pair of shorts, and black boots. A purple satin cape is draped on one shoulder to signify allegiance to the throne. You'll be sure to win the cosplay battle with your morning star weapon as you fight for riches, for glory, or just for the sake of the fight!

Centurion Gladiator Costume Pieces

Armor. 72
Cape. 60
Leg Guards 92
Arm Guards 92
Morning Star. 76

Centurion Gladiator **Armor**

Shopping List

- Household foam
- EVA foam
- Sew-on hook-and-loop tape
- Eight ⅝" washers
- 54 concho studs
- Two 1½" grommets
- 2 belts
- Leather lace
- Rub n' Buff® in gold and silver

Tools

- Ceramic or steel bowl
- 2 large binder clips
- Tape measure
- Scissors
- Tailor's chalk
- Heat-resistant gloves
- Face mask
- Heat gun
- Hot glue gun and glue sticks
- Woodburning tool

Here is a basic project of full body armor to help you get started with foam and take your cosplay to the next level!

1. **Cut the foam.** Measure the cosplayer around the chest and shoulders with their arms down. This measurement will be the circumference (outside edge) of the circle you'll need for the pauldrons. Cut a circle with the circumference you measured from household foam.

2. **Begin shaping the foam.** Find a steel or ceramic bowl that is similar in size to the foam circle you cut. Working in a well-ventilated space with heat-resistant gloves and a face mask, place the foam inside the bowl and use a heat gun to shape the foam to match the curve of the bowl.

3. **Add the waves.** Fold the foam circle in half. Use the heat gun to form waves to each side of the fold as shown.

. **Cut the foam.** Let the foam cool, then cut the circle into two matching half-circles. Cut the pieces so the waves are positioned at the corners of each half-circle.

5. **Shape the shoulders.** At the top of each pauldron, where the curve for the shoulder is, cut two 3" slits parallel to each other and 2½" apart to create a tab. Lift the tab and bring the two edges of the shoulder piece together underneath it. Hot glue the edges together, using binder clips to hold them in place while the glue cools. Then glue the tab in place on top.

6. **Add the ties.** Punch holes in the corner of each pauldron with a pointed woodburning tool. Hot glue washers over the front and back of each hole. Thread leather lace through the holes to create closures.

7. **Add the medallions.** Cut two 3" x 1½" rectangles from the foam. Glue a rectangle diagonally to the front of each pauldron, positioning one end of the rectangle at the front corner. Cut two 3"-diameter circles from the foam for medallions. Hot glue a medallion at the other end of each rectangle, trimming the pieces as necessary to fit. Use a pointed woodburning tool to emboss the medallions as shown.

8. **Add the studs.** Attach concho studs to the edges of the pauldrons and the center of the medallions. Use the eraser end of a pencil to fold down the legs of the studs to secure them in place.

9. **Create the stitching.** Use the woodburning tool to emboss the pauldrons around the edges to create faux stitching. Take two grommets and hot glue a concho stud to the center of each one. Then glue a grommet on top of the shoulder tab of each pauldron.

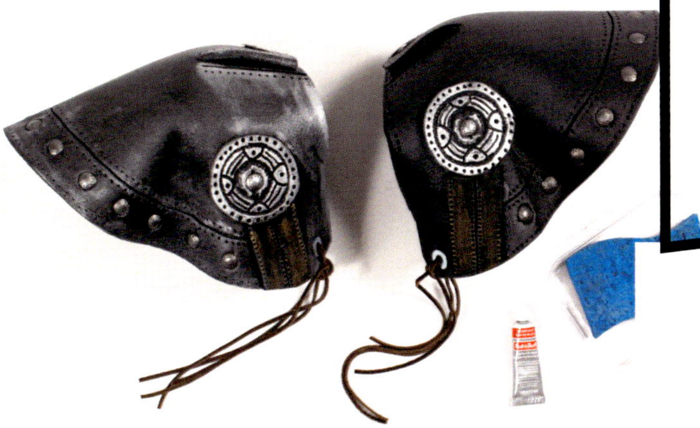

10. **Add color.** Apply gold Rub n' Buff® to the rectangles on the front of the pauldrons to make them resemble leather straps. Lightly apply silver Rub n' Buff® to the other areas of the pauldrons. Use a damp sponge to blend the silver over the armor to resemble aged leather. Apply a heavier coat of silver Rub n' Buff® to the medallions to highlight the raised areas.

11. **Make the chest piece.** For the chest piece, measure the cosplayer to determine the width and length you need. Using the measurements, cut the chest piece from EVA foam. Use a heat tool to give the foam the appearance of a "6-pack." Add faux stitching with a woodburning tool and paint the chest piece as you did the pauldrons. Cut vertical slits in the top corners and along each side so you can attach the chest piece using two crisscrossed belts.

12. **Make the arm and leg guards.** For the arm and leg guards, measure the cosplayer to determine the width and length you need. For this costume, the guards curve around the top of the arms and legs instead of wrapping all the way around. Using the measurements, cut the pieces from EVA foam. Use heat to shape the pieces into curves. Embellish and paint the pieces as you did for the pauldrons and chest piece. Use hook-and-loop tape to create straps to attach the arm and leg guards.

Centurion Gladiator **Morning Star**

Shopping List

- Bicycle tire inner tube (butyl rubber or latex)
- 16"-long ⅝" PVC pipe
- 5" foam ball
- 2 washers
- 3" screw with bolt
- Party noisemakers

Tools

- Zip ties
- Hot glue gun and glue sticks

1. **Wrap the pipe.** Cover the pipe with strips of inner tube, using zip ties to secure the ends. Cut the mouthpieces off the noisemakers and push them into the foam ball to form spikes.

2. **Wrap the ball.** Cover the foam ball with strips of inner tube, using hot glue to secure the ends.

3. **Finish the end.** Bind or glue several thin strips of inner tube together to form a tassel. Push the end of the tassel into the end of the pipe. Slide the washers onto the screw and use the bolt to hold them in place at the top. Push the screw into the end of the pipe with the tassel.

4. **Finish.** Push the other end of the pipe into the foam ball. Add hot glue for extra security if needed.

Top-Tier Ninja

You'll upgrade to Tier 5 when you wear this ninja costume to your next cosplay event. The mask is hand-painted and has foam ears. The gold quilted jacket is made from a furniture moving blanket and accented with fuchsia duct tape. The basic undergarments are black sweats and a sleeveless fuchsia hoodie worn over a black t-shirt. The tennis shoes are topped with foam pieces trimmed with gold and white duct tape. With a foam board and duct tape pickaxe in hand, you'll journey into the unknown, piercing through to a higher plane in this fierce costume!

Top-Tier Ninja Costume Pieces

Fingerless Gloves 80

Coat 82

Mask......................... 84

Pickaxe...................... 86

Use these instructions to create the gloves for the Woodland Fox using tan felt and faux fur trim.

Use these instructions to create the gloves for the Unicorn Fairy using white faux fur.

Top-Tier Ninja Fingerless Gloves

Shopping List

- ⅓ yd black pleather
- Matching thread
- Gold OlyFun™ fabric

Tools

- Tape measure
- Scissors
- Pins
- Fabric glue

This simple cosplay accessory is super-quick to make. These basic fingerless gloves can be adapted for many other costumes. Use white faux fur for the Unicorn Fairy, tan felt with a strip of brown faux fur for the Woodland Fox, black faux leather for the Sea God, and brown faux leather for the American Superhero. The instructions here are for the Top-Tier Ninja fingerless gloves, which are made longer than the others to form cuffs. Gold patches are added to coordinate with the gold on the rest of the costume.

1. **Cut the fabric.** To determine the width of the gloves, measure the cosplayer's hand by wrapping a measuring tape completely around the thumb and knuckles, then add 1" for the seam and ease. For the length of the gloves, measure from the knuckles to the wrist, then add 6" for the cuffs. Use the pattern on page 110 and the measurements to cut the glove pieces from the pleather.

2. **Sew the gloves.** Fold each glove in half with right sides facing and pin in place. Sew a ½" seam along the long side of each glove.

3. **Sew the thumbs.** Turn the gloves right side out. Sew the thumb seam in each one by stitching 1" from the point of each glove as marked on the pattern.

4. **Form the cuffs.** For gloves with a cuff, fold down the end of each glove 3".

5. **Add the gold accents.** Cut two 2" x 3" rectangles from gold OlyFun™ fabric and glue one rectangle to the top of each glove with fabric glue.

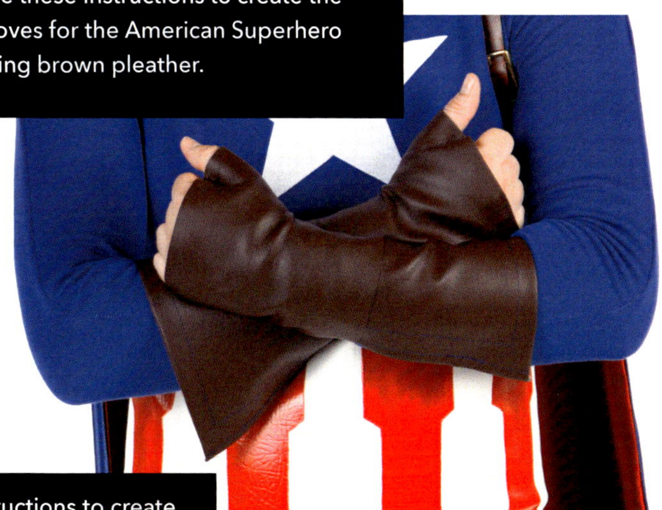

Use these instructions to create the gloves for the American Superhero using brown pleather.

Use these instructions to create the gloves for the Sea God using black pleather.

Top-Tier Ninja **Coat**

Shopping List

- Quilted furniture mover's blanket
- Gold Aluminor™ thermal fabric
- Duct tape in gold and fuchsia
- Black thread

Tools

- Spray adhesive
- Tape measure
- Scissors
- Pins

A kimono is a traditional Japanese-style garment that can add so much to a cosplayer's ensemble, like this one for the Top-Tier Ninja. The fabric is unconventional—a quilted furniture mover's blanket. These blankets are large and relatively inexpensive, making them a great value. To complete the look, additional quilted material purchased at the craft store is added to the front of the coat, and fuchsia and gold duct tape are used to cover the raw edges and add accent trim. The size of the coat is determined by the measurements of the cosplayer. This piece requires more advanced sewing skills.

1. **Cut the back of the coat.** To determine the length of the coat, measure the cosplayer from the nape of the neck to the back of the knee. For the width at the top of the coat, measure from shoulder to shoulder. For the width at the bottom of the coat, add 6" to the shoulder measurement. Using the diagram on page 111 and the measurements, cut the piece for the back of the coat from the mover's blanket. Cut the bottom of the coat into a 12"-tall V shape.

2. **Cut the front of the coat.** Follow the diagram on page 111 to cut the piece for the front of the coat using the same measurements that you did for the back of the coat. Invert the shape at the bottom so it forms a 12"-tall triangle instead of a V. Cut from each side of the neck to the center line at the waist. Then cut along the center line from the waist to the bottom to separate the front piece into two panels.

3. **Cut the sleeves.** To determine the length of the sleeves, measure the cosplayer from shoulder to elbow. The sleeves are 20" wide at the top and 36" wide at the bottom. Use the diagram on page 111 and the length measurement to cut the sleeves from the mover's blanket.

4. **Sew the coat.** With right sides facing, sew the front panels to the back of the coat at the shoulders with 1" seams. Pleat the top of each sleeve following the pattern. Sew on the sleeves, matching the pleats on each sleeve to the shoulder seams of the coat. Then sew the side seams of the coat together.

5. **Add the gold fabric.** Cut two pieces of the gold Aluminor™ fabric to fit the front of the coat. Use spray adhesive to attach them to the coat. Cover the edges of the Aluminor™ with gold duct tape.

6. **Finish the edges.** Cover the edges of the coat and sleeves with gold duct tape.

7. **Add the accents.** Use additional gold duct tape and fuchsia duct tape to embellish the sleeves and the neck of the coat. For narrow strips of duct tape, tear a piece of duct tape from the roll, and then tear it in half down the center before adding it to the coat.

Top-Tier Ninja **Mask**

Shopping List

- White plastic craft mask with elastic strap
- White craft foam
- Gold metallic paint pen
- Fuchsia acrylic paint
- Black permanent marker

Tools

- Craft knife
- Pencil
- Scissors
- Paintbrushes
- Stapler
- Hot glue gun and glue sticks
- Clothespins

1. **Shape the eyes.** Remove the elastic from the back of the mask. Using a craft knife, cut the corners of the eyes into curved Vs as shown.

2. **Draw the design.** Sketch your paint design on the mask with a pencil.

3. **Paint the design.** Apply the fuchsia paint with a fine-point paintbrush and let it dry. Then add the metallic gold paint with a paint pen and let it dry. Draw the design for the mouth with a black permanent marker.

4. **Cut the foam.** Using the pattern on page 112, cut two inner ears and two outer ears from the white foam.

5. **Shape the ears.** Paint the inner ears fuchsia and let dry. Glue the inner ears on top of the outer ears. Pinch the base of each ear together and staple in place as shown.

6. **Attach the ears.** Hot glue the ears to the top edge of the mask. If needed, use clothespins to hold the ears in place while the glue cools. Reattach the elastic strap to the mask.

Top-Tier Ninja **Pickaxe**

Shopping List

- 32"-long 1½" metal pipe
- Foam core board
- Duct tape in fuchsia and gold
- Fuchsia spray paint
- Metallic gold cardstock
- Thumbtacks
- Gold chain
- Black craft foam

Tools

- Scissors
- Glue

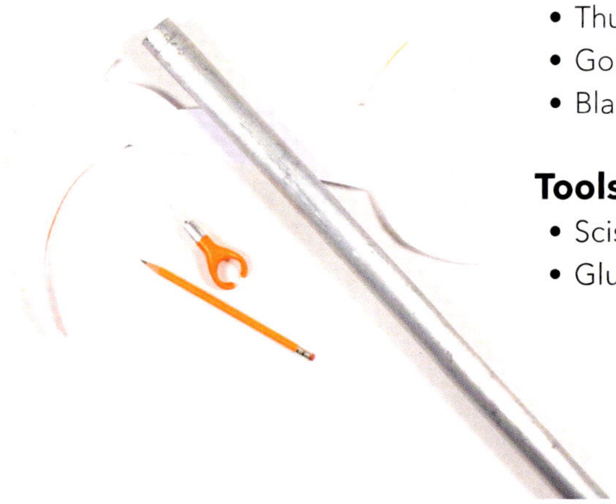

1. **Cut the foam board.** Use the pattern on page 113 to cut out two copies of the pickaxe blade from the foam core board.

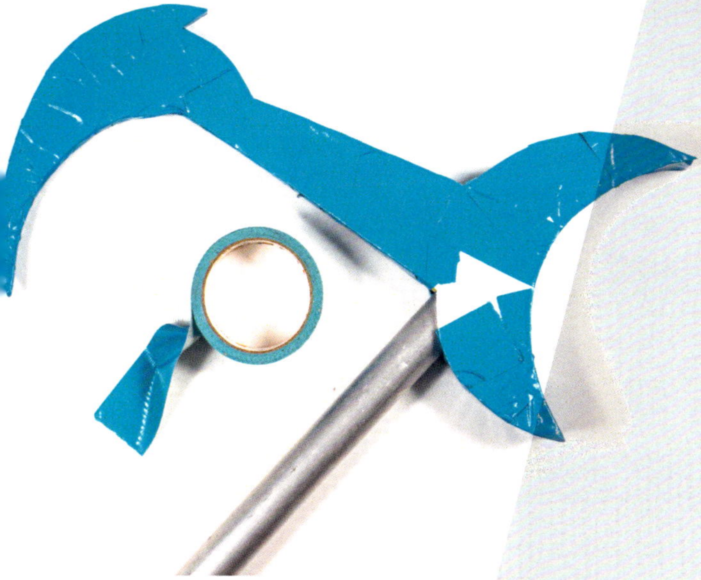

2. **Tape the blade.** Place the pipe handle between the two pickaxe cutouts and tape the cutouts together with duct tape.

3. **Add the cardstock.** In a well-ventilated area, spray-paint the pickaxe fuchsia and let it dry. Cut out two lightning bolts from the cardstock and glue one on each side of the pickaxe. Add thumbtacks to the lightning bolts to resemble rivets.

4. **Finish.** Add small lightning bolts in fuchsia duct tape to both sides of the pickaxe blade. Tape a chain to the bottom of the pipe with gold duct tape and wrap the pipe with gold tape. Wrap the bottom of the pipe with black foam. Add pink duct tape diamonds to the pipe above the foam.

Sea God

Sea God Costume Pieces

Pauldrons 90

Arm, Leg & Thigh Wraps 92

Waist Cincher 66

Staff......................... 96

From the depths of the sea came this cosplay character who is angry and ready to fight as half-human and half-Atlantean. A black long-sleeve t-shirt and leggings are the base of this costume. A furniture moving blanket is transformed into the soft body armor, which has been sprayed with gold and bronze fabric paint. The armor is completed with pauldrons, a waist cincher, armbands, and leg wraps. Black pleather fingerless gloves, black boots, and a black belt with a golden shell glued on as a buckle finish off the outfit. The final piece is a staff, complete with real seashells, for our protector of the deep and god of the sea!

Sea God **Pauldrons**

Shopping List

- Quilted furniture mover's blanket
- Matching thread
- Heavy cardstock
- Fabric spray paint in gold and bronze
- Sew-on hook-and-loop tape

Tools

- Tape measure
- Scissors
- Pins
- Tailor's chalk

Pauldrons are domed pieces of armor made to protect the shoulders that date back to the fifteenth century. For cosplay, they can be made from numerous materials like foam, metal, or quilted furniture moving pads. The Sea God costume includes pauldrons made from furniture moving pads to give the design a strong silhouette. The pauldrons are painted to add visual texture. The same pattern used for this costume could also be used to create pauldrons from thin foam for other characters.

1. **Cut the fabric.** To determine the width of the bodice, measure from shoulder to shoulder. Use the pattern on page 114 and the shoulder measurement to cut the bodice and two pauldron pieces from the fabric. For the bodice, cut along the solid lines only. Mark the dashed lines on the top of the bodice with tailor's chalk.

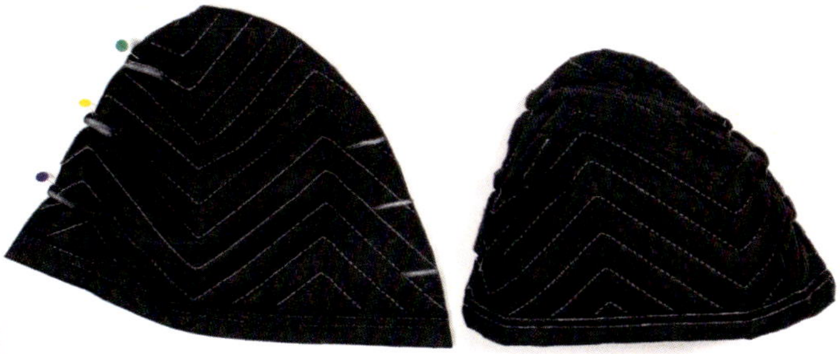

2. **Sew the pleats.** With right sides facing, pin and sew ½" pleats in each pauldron at the (-) symbols marked on the pattern.

3. **Attach the pauldrons.** Place the pauldrons on top of the bodice, matching up the carrot (<) symbols marked on the patterns. Sew the pauldrons to the bodice using a zigzag stitch. Also zigzag stitch along the raw edges of the pauldrons and bodice to prevent fraying.

4. **Paint the pauldrons.** Using the pattern on page 115, cut the shark tooth stencil from heavy cardstock. Place the stencil at the top of one shoulder and spray along the edge with bronze paint. Move the stencil down the shoulder and spray along the edge with gold. Repeat, alternating colors until both shoulders have been covered. Leave the front unpainted. Let it dry.

5. **Paint the back.** For the back, place the stencil in the center of the armor and spray along the edge with gold paint. Move the stencil up and spray along the edge with bronze paint. Repeat, alternating colors until the entire piece has been painted. Let it dry.

6. **Add the closure.** Sew or glue hook-and-loop tape to the front corners of the bodice as shown for a closure.

Sea God **Arm, Leg & Thigh Wraps**

Shopping List

- 1 yd heavy-weight fabric
- Matching thread
- Fabric spray paint in gold and bronze
- Sew-on hook-and-loop tape
- Heavy cardstock

Tools

- Tape measure
- Scissors
- Pins
- Tailor's chalk

There are tons of costumes that you can enhance with arm, leg, or thigh wraps. They're really quick and easy to make! Simply measure around your legs and arms to get the perfect fit. The fabric and materials you use will make your wraps unique for each character. Add faux fur or lace trim, rhinestones, patches of color, or paint them. A simple stencil and spray paint were used to make the shark-tooth pattern on the Sea God's wraps.

Use these instructions to create the leg wraps for the American Superhero using brown pleather.

Use these instructions to create leg wraps for the Unicorn Fairy using white faux fur.

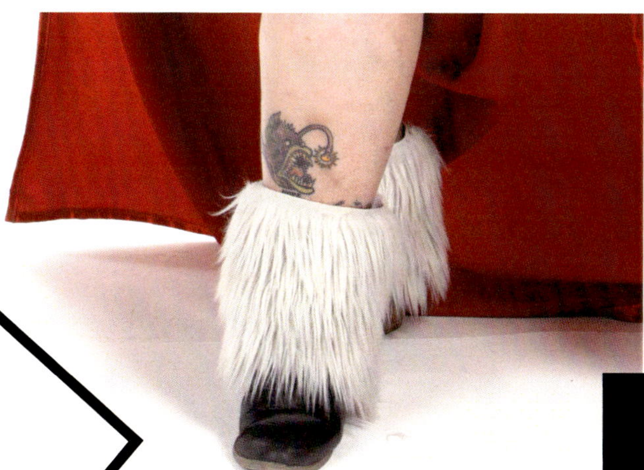

Use these instructions to create the arm and leg wraps for the Nordic Princess using black pleather and fur trim.

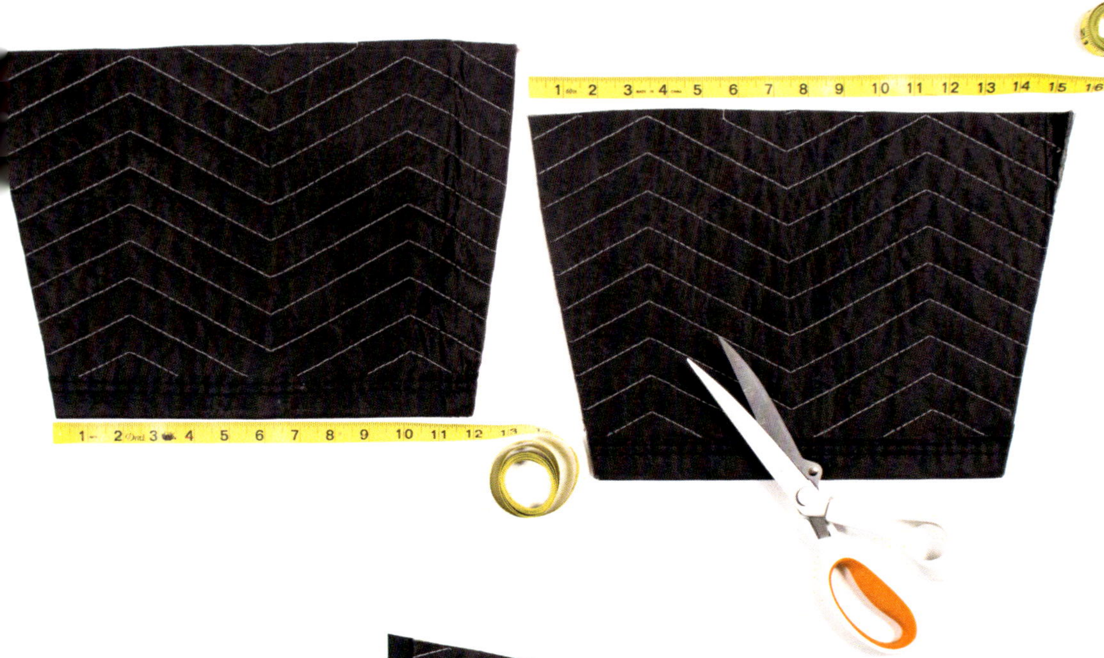

1. **Cut the fabric.** For the arm wraps, measure around the cosplayer's wrist to determine the width of the narrow end and around the cosplayer's arm below the elbow to determine the width of the wide end. Measure from elbow to wrist for the length. For the leg wraps, measure around the ankle, around the leg below the knee, and from knee to ankle. For the thigh wraps, measure around the top of the knee, around the leg below the crotch, and from crotch to knee. If you plan to hem the pieces, add 1½" to each measurement. Mark and cut all the pieces from the fabric.

2. **Finish the edges.** To hem the pieces, fold each side under ¾" and topstitch. For fabrics that will fray but are too thick to hem, use the exact measurements from Step 1 to cut out the pieces and serge or zigzag stitch around the edges to prevent fraying.

3. **Paint.** Using the pattern on page 115, cut the shark tooth stencil from heavy cardstock. Place the stencil on top of each piece and spray along the edge with bronze paint. Move the stencil down and spray along the edge with gold. Repeat, alternating colors until you've created the pattern you want.

4. **Add closures.** Sew or hot glue pieces of hook and loop tape to the long edges of each wrap to create closures.

Sea God **Staff**

Shopping List

- Broom handle
- Black pleather (optional)
- Large seashells
- Black cord
- 2" x 9" x ½" piece of wood
- Zip ties
- Black spray paint
- Gold Rub n' Buff®

Tools

- Two-part epoxy
- Scissors
- Hot glue gun and glue sticks
- Power drill

1. **Wrap the handle.** Working in a well-ventilated area, spray-paint the broom handle and let it dry. Starting 11" from the top of the broom handle, wrap black cord around the handle, covering 6". Secure the ends with hot glue.

2. **Paint the decorations.** Spray-paint the shells and wood piece black and let them dry.

3. **Attach the wood piece.** Drill a hole in each corner of the wood piece. Use zip ties and the drilled holes to attach the wood to the top of the broom handle above the cording. Trim off the ends of the zip ties.

4. **Attach the shells.** Lightly apply gold Rub n' Buff® to the raised areas of the seashells and let them dry. Use two-part epoxy to attach the shells to the wood piece and let them dry. If desired, tie on strips of black pleather.

We had a lot of fun with this look and really went wild with it, using a gold metallic lip paint to create a faux mask. Experiment with black and white eyeshadow to create lines and dots along the outer brow and under the mask to help bring this look together.

Makeup

For some cosplayers, makeup is an integral part of their costume. Makeup is also very particular to the individual. Consider using gemstones, artificial eyelashes, metallic finishes, glitter, stencils, and other makeup to enhance your cosplay experience.

Test your makeup ideas before your big day and get comfortable with all of the different products so you can feel confident in your application skills. There are great tutorials online for cosplay makeup techniques that define your character. By experimenting and trying new techniques, colors, and looks, you'll find what works for you.

In addition to makeup, adding eye contacts, wigs, and hair accessories can enhance your character even more. These pieces are easy to find in specialty stores and online.

Use your inspiration board to collect makeup ideas to help guide your makeup application and color choices. It takes a bit of work to achieve those anime eyes or create perfect facial contours, but it will be worth it when you portray your character and the cameras start clicking! Check out the photos in this section to see the makeup used for the 8 cosplays in this workbook.

Heavy moisturizer was used to get that dewy glow. A heavy hand on the dark eyeshadow gives the Sea God his smoldering stare, with a touch of gold on the outer brow to emphasize his royal status.

This look is simple to create, but anything but basic. We went with pink tones on the lips and cheeks and used an eyeliner pen to draw in thick, spaced out eyelashes along the bottom of the eye. Falsies along the top complete the look.

Basic Cosplay Makeup Kit

- Moisturizer
- Foundation
- Concealer
- Base powder
- Highlighter
- Contouring powder
- Blush
- Eye shadow primer
- Eye shadows
- Eyeliner pens
- Artificial eyelashes
- Eyelash glue
- Mascara
- Eyebrow pencils
- Lip liners
- Lipsticks
- Lip glosses
- Finishing spray
- Makeup sponges
- Cotton swabs
- Tweezers
- Makeup brushes
- Makeup remover

False eyelashes really make this look pop. We used warm tones on the eyes to create a smoky cat eye and continued with golden orange on the lips with a metallic matte lip paint. To create the whiskers, we used the same metallic lip paint and added black eyeliner along the undersides to give definition.

To achieve this look, we went with cool tones, using a bluish-purple eyeshadow on the eyes and matte lip paint on the lips. A light highlighter was used on the cheeks to give that ethereal glow. For a fun touch, use body crystals along the top brow line to sparkle and shine!

Patterns

Unicorn Headdress Pattern

Photocopy at 130% or at size needed for cosplayer.

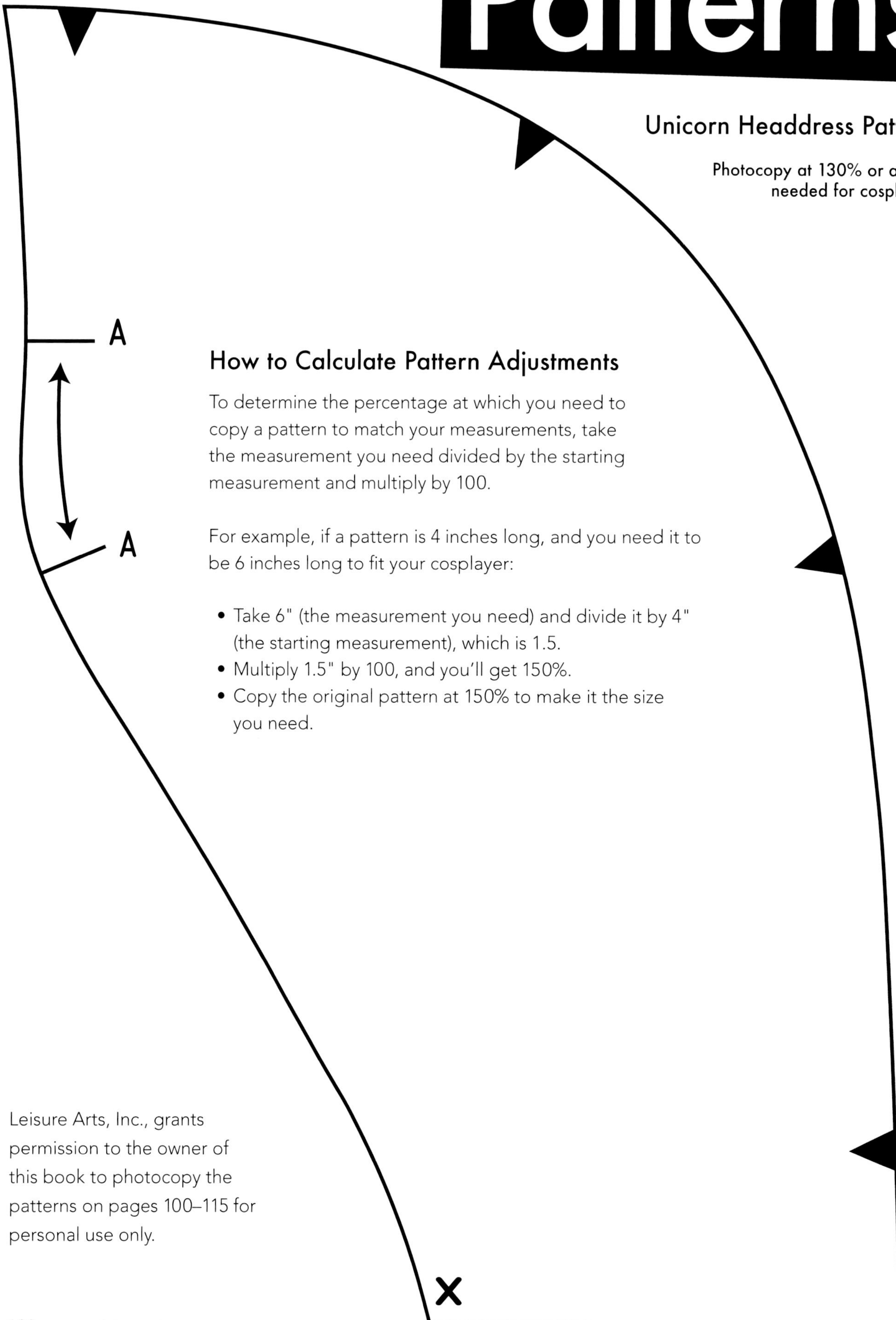

How to Calculate Pattern Adjustments

To determine the percentage at which you need to copy a pattern to match your measurements, take the measurement you need divided by the starting measurement and multiply by 100.

For example, if a pattern is 4 inches long, and you need it to be 6 inches long to fit your cosplayer:

- Take 6" (the measurement you need) and divide it by 4" (the starting measurement), which is 1.5.
- Multiply 1.5" by 100, and you'll get 150%.
- Copy the original pattern at 150% to make it the size you need.

Unicorn Wings Pattern

Photocopy at 180% for actual size.

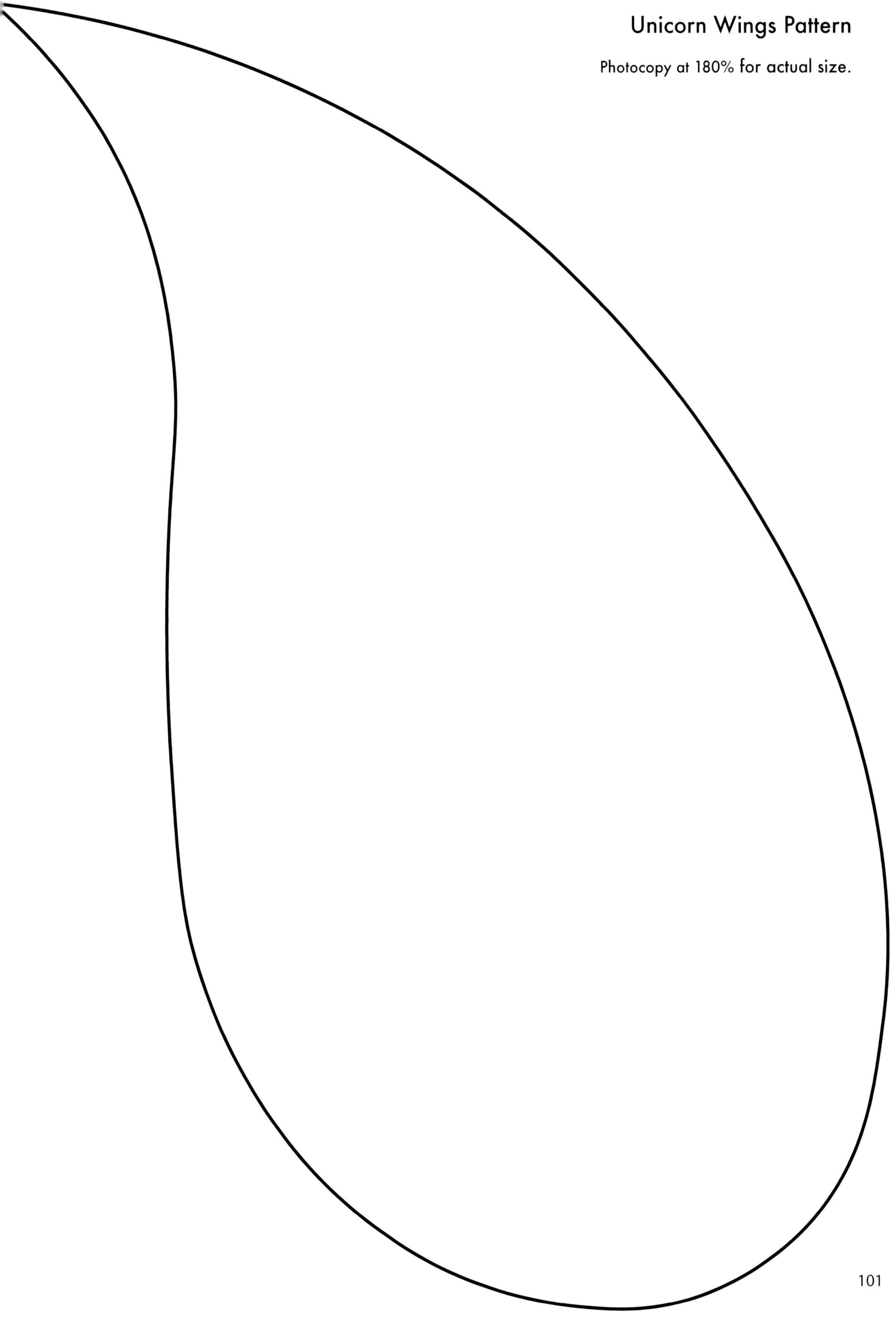

Unicorn Ears Pattern

Pattern shown at actual size.

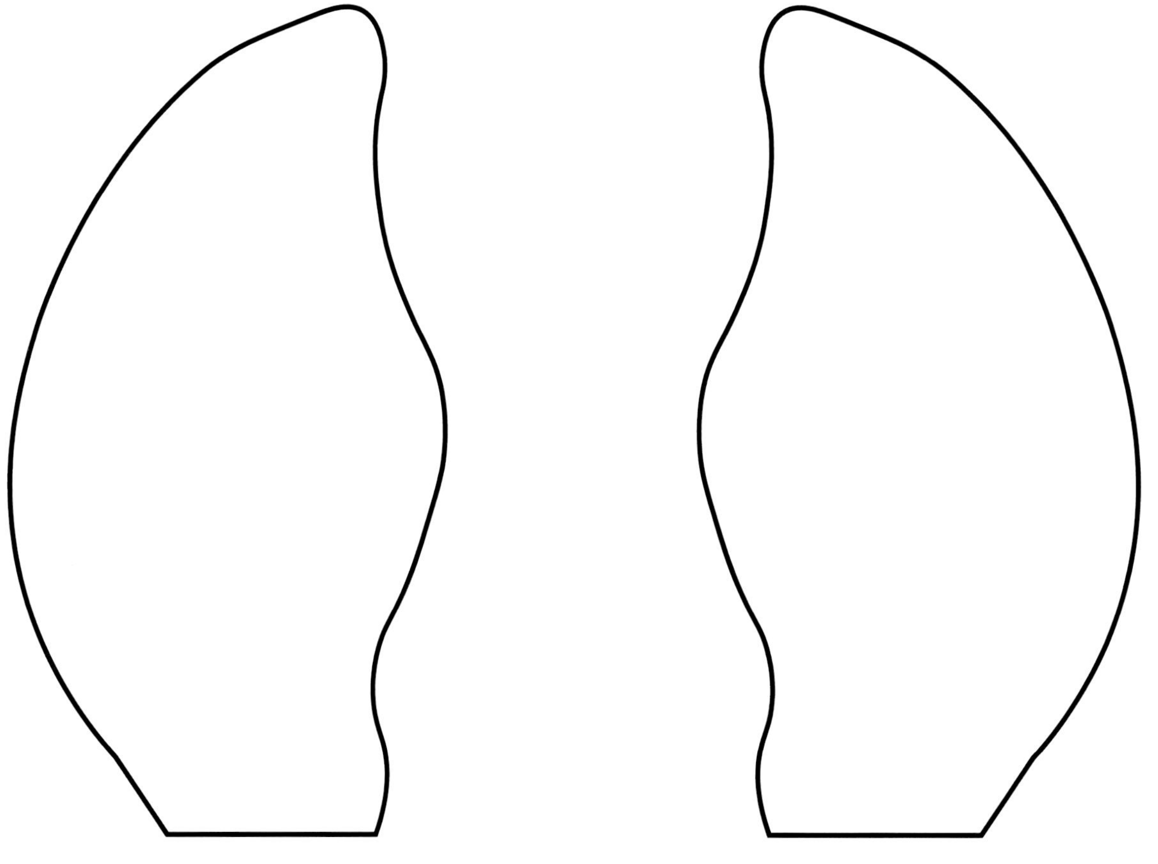

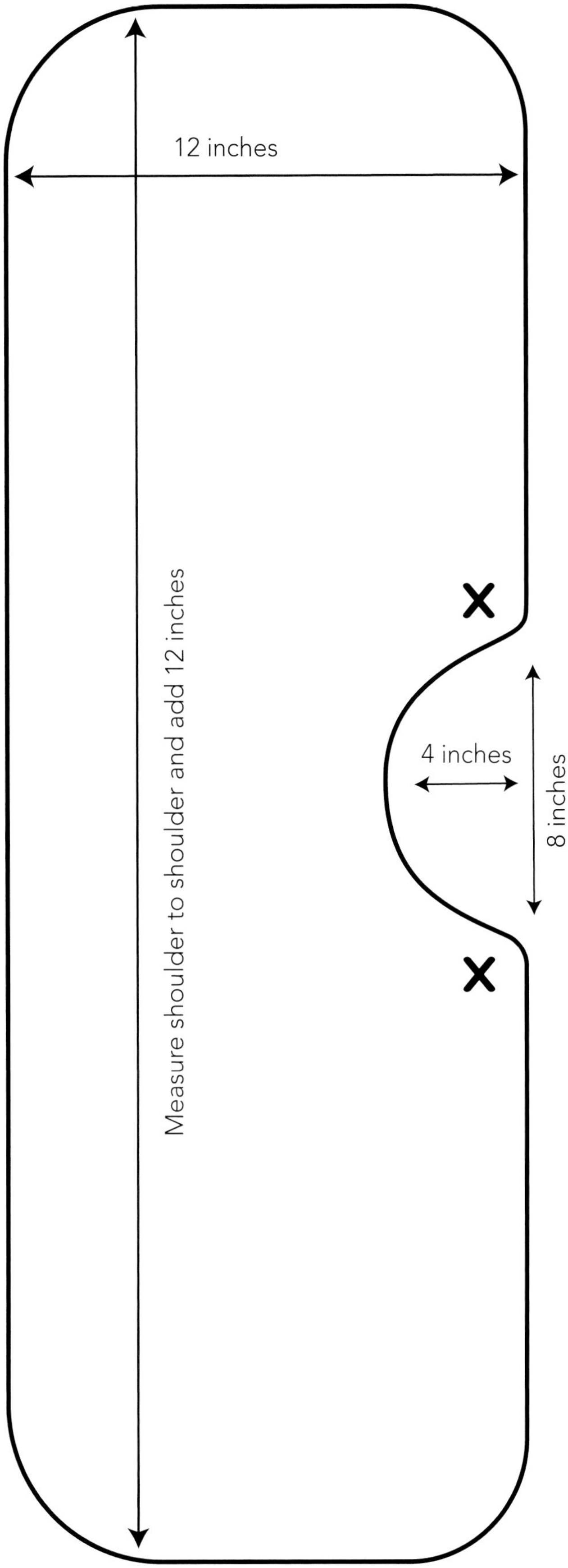
12 inches
Measure shoulder to shoulder and add 12 inches
4 inches
8 inches

Woodland Fox Tail Pattern

Photocopy at 240% or at size needed for cosplayer.

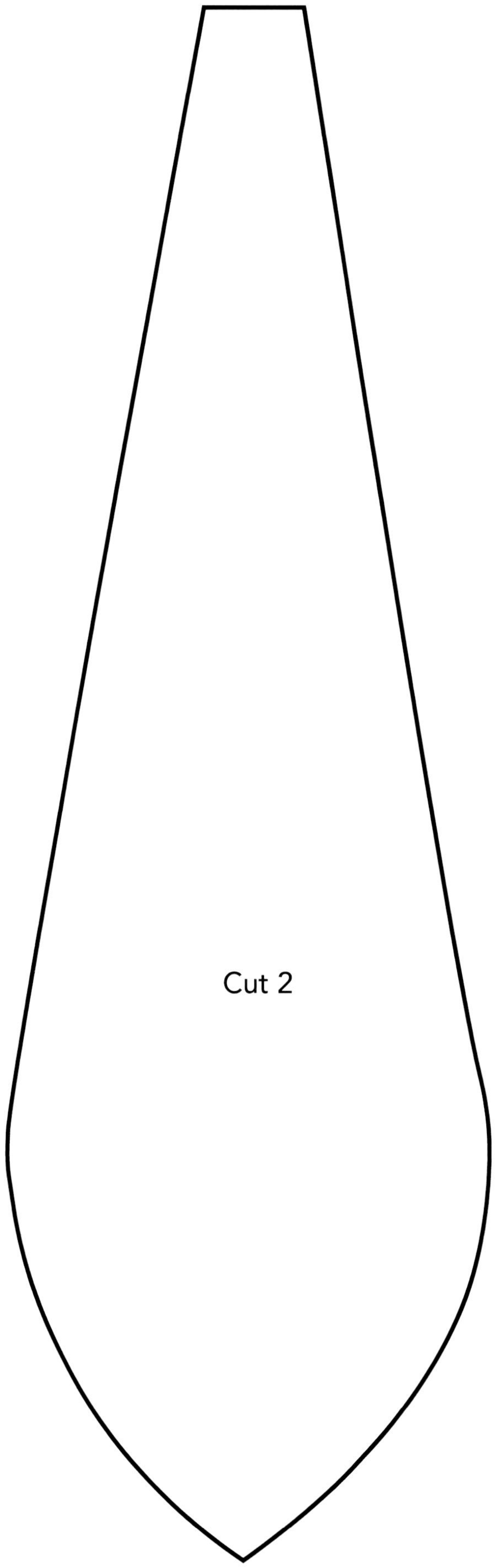

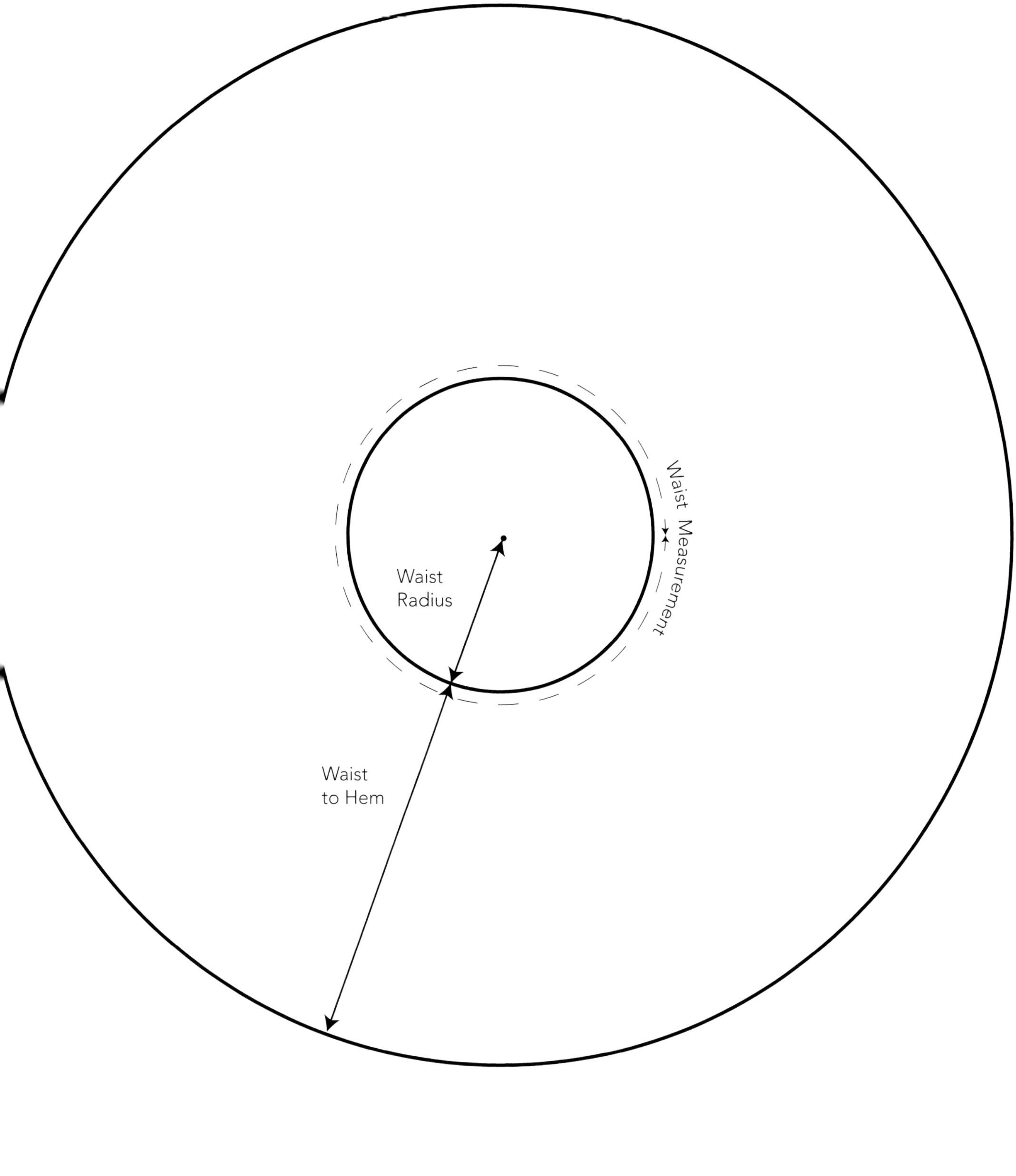
Waist Measurement
Waist
Radius
Waist
to Hem

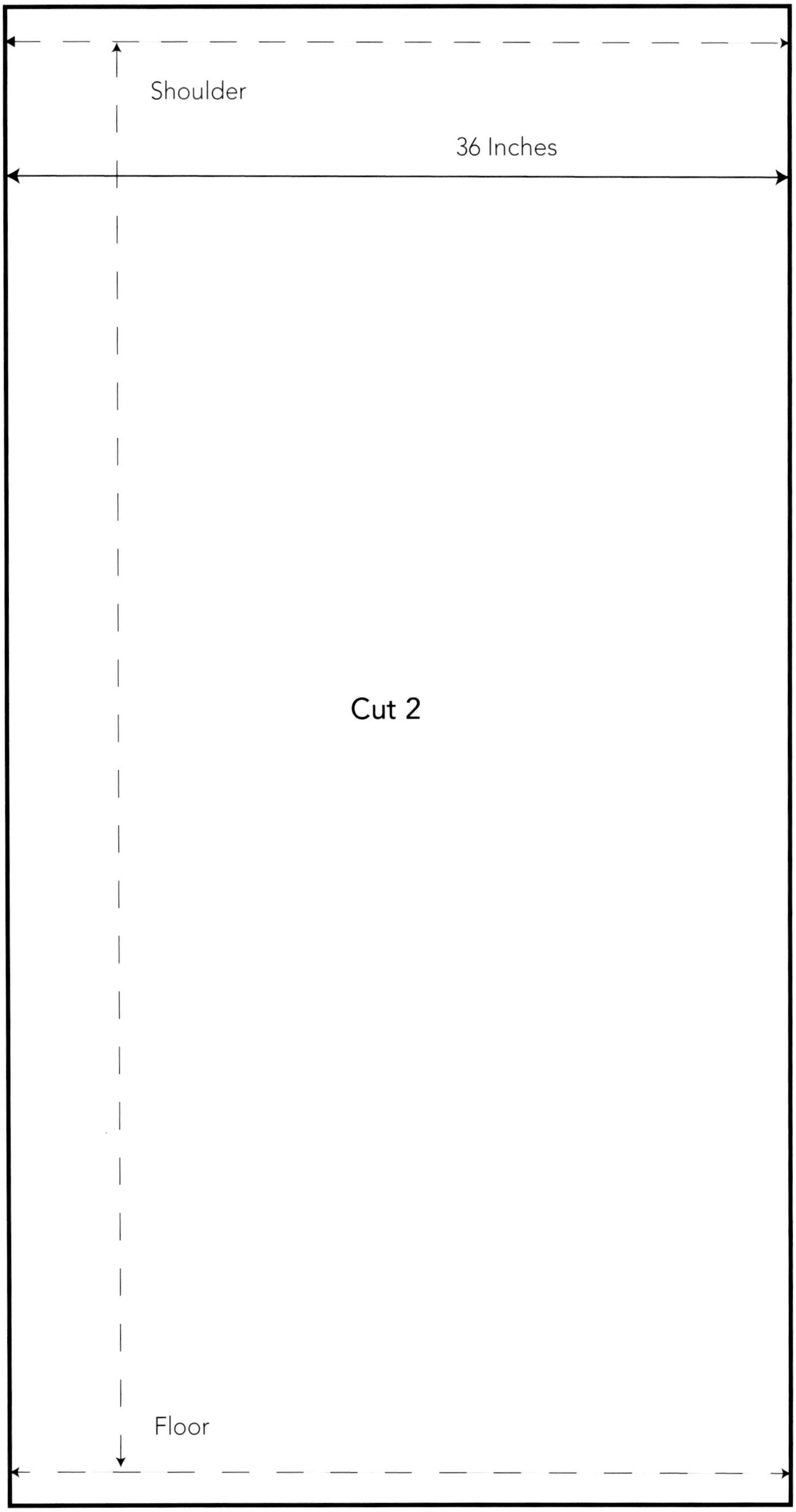
Shoulder
36 Inches
Cut 2
Floor

Cap Pattern

Photocopy at 190% or at size needed for cosplayer.

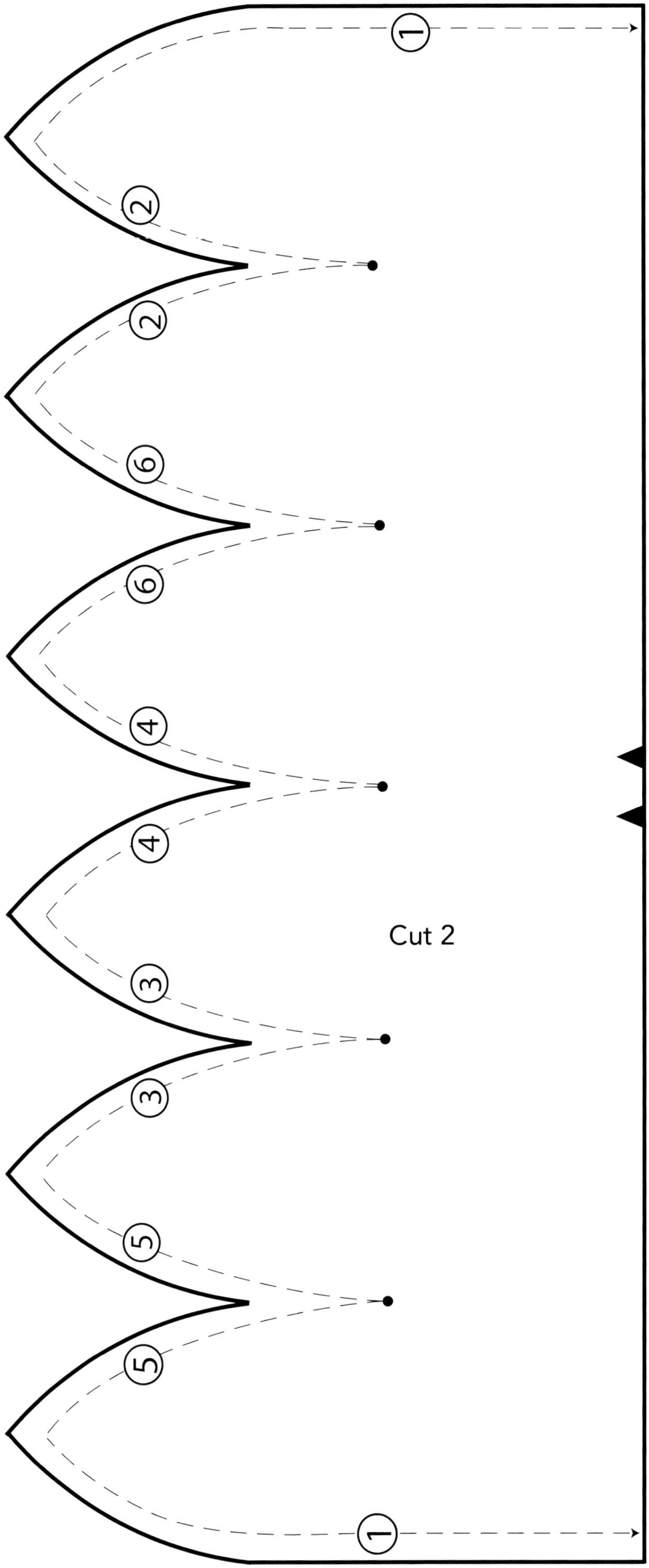

Mask Pattern

Pattern shown at actual size.

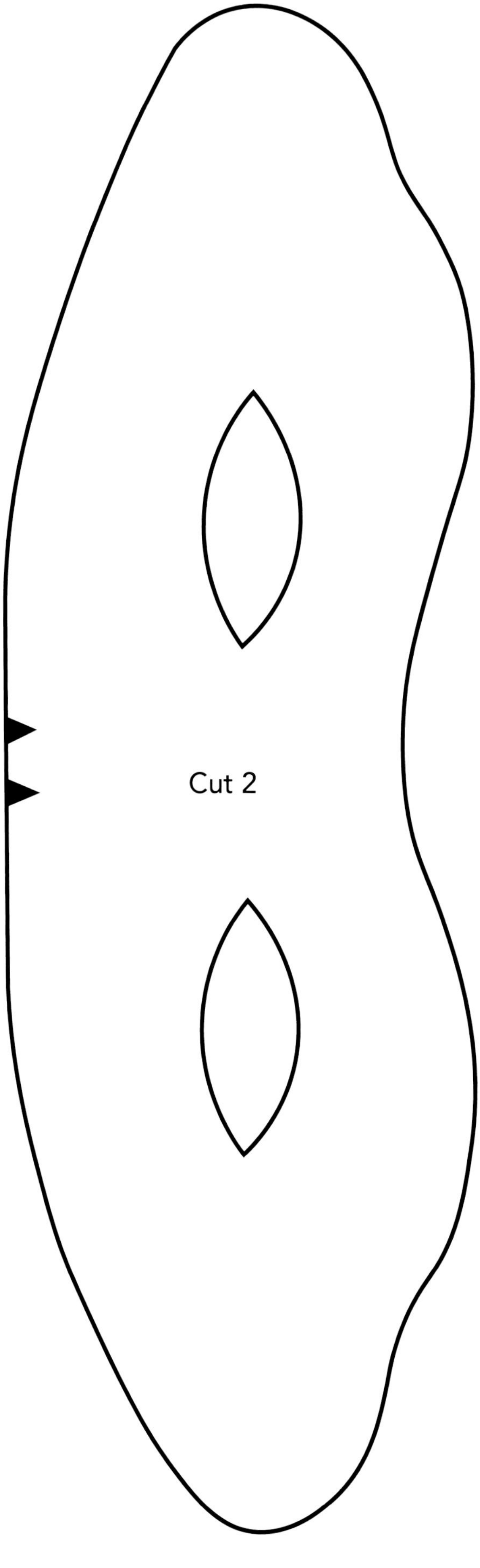

5-Point Star Pattern

Photocopy at 120% for actual size.

Fingerless Glove Patter

Pattern shown a
actual size. Adjust t
size of cosplaye
as needed

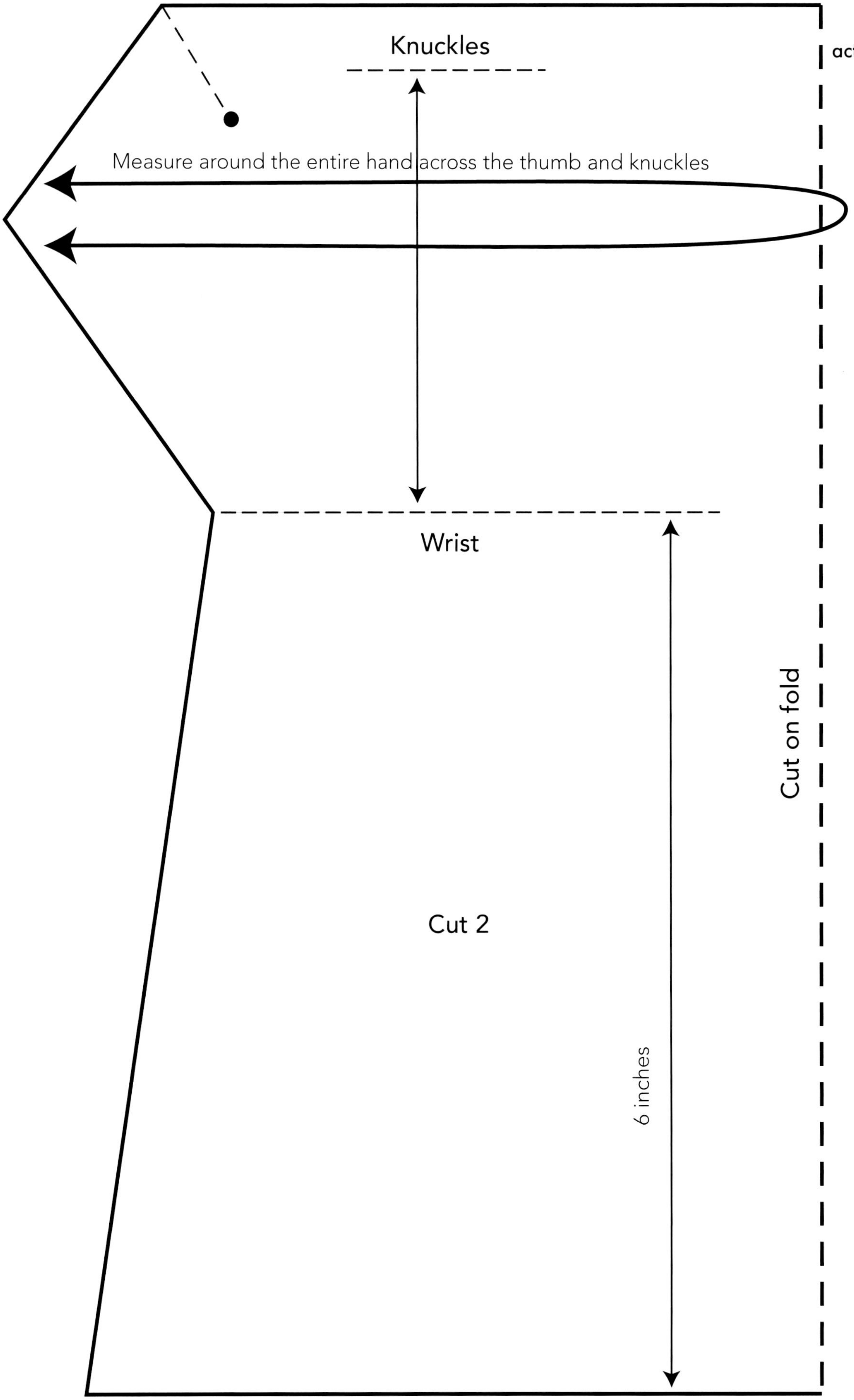

Ninja Coat Pattern

Photocopy at 800% or at size needed for cosplayer.

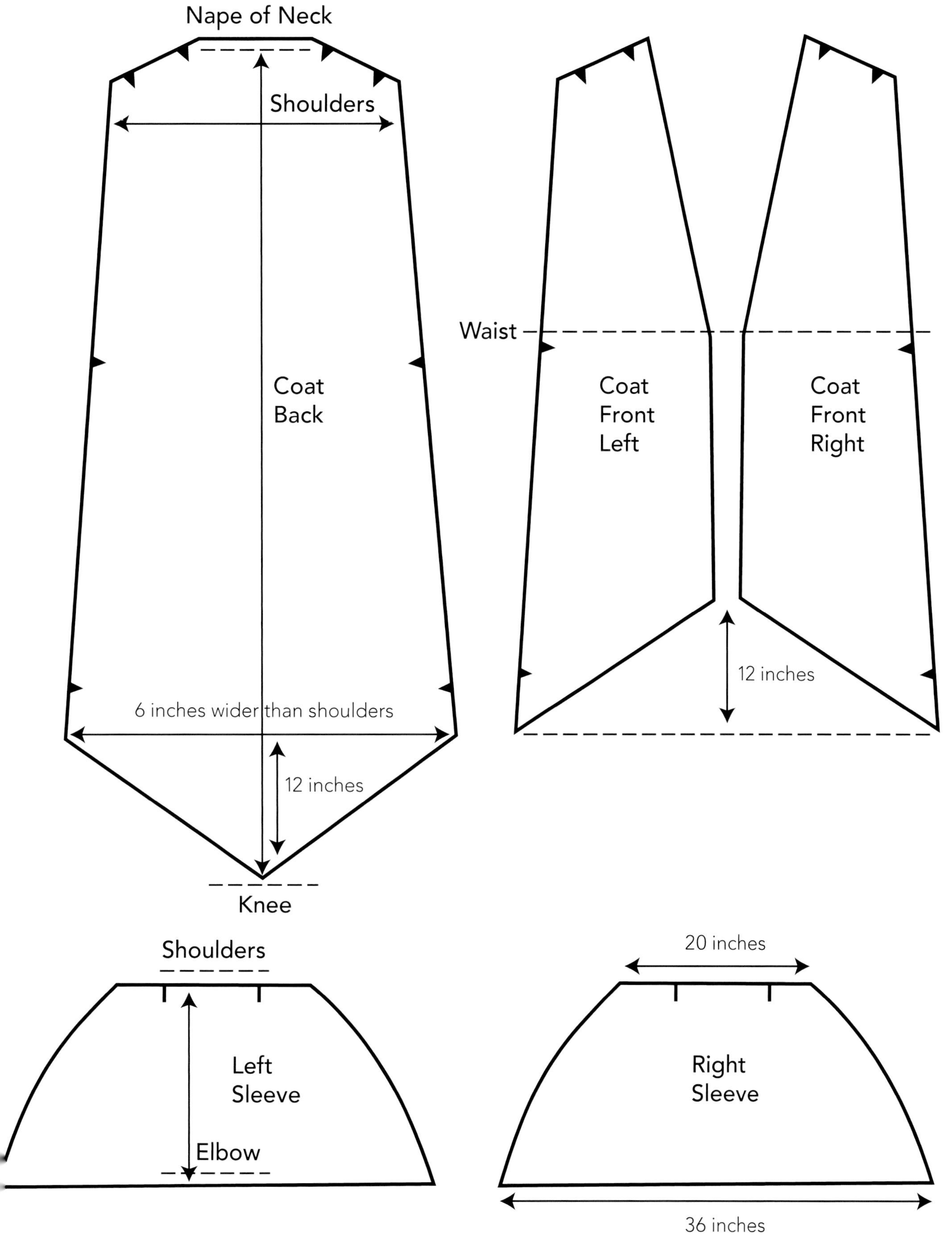

Ninja Ears Pattern

Pattern shown at actual size.

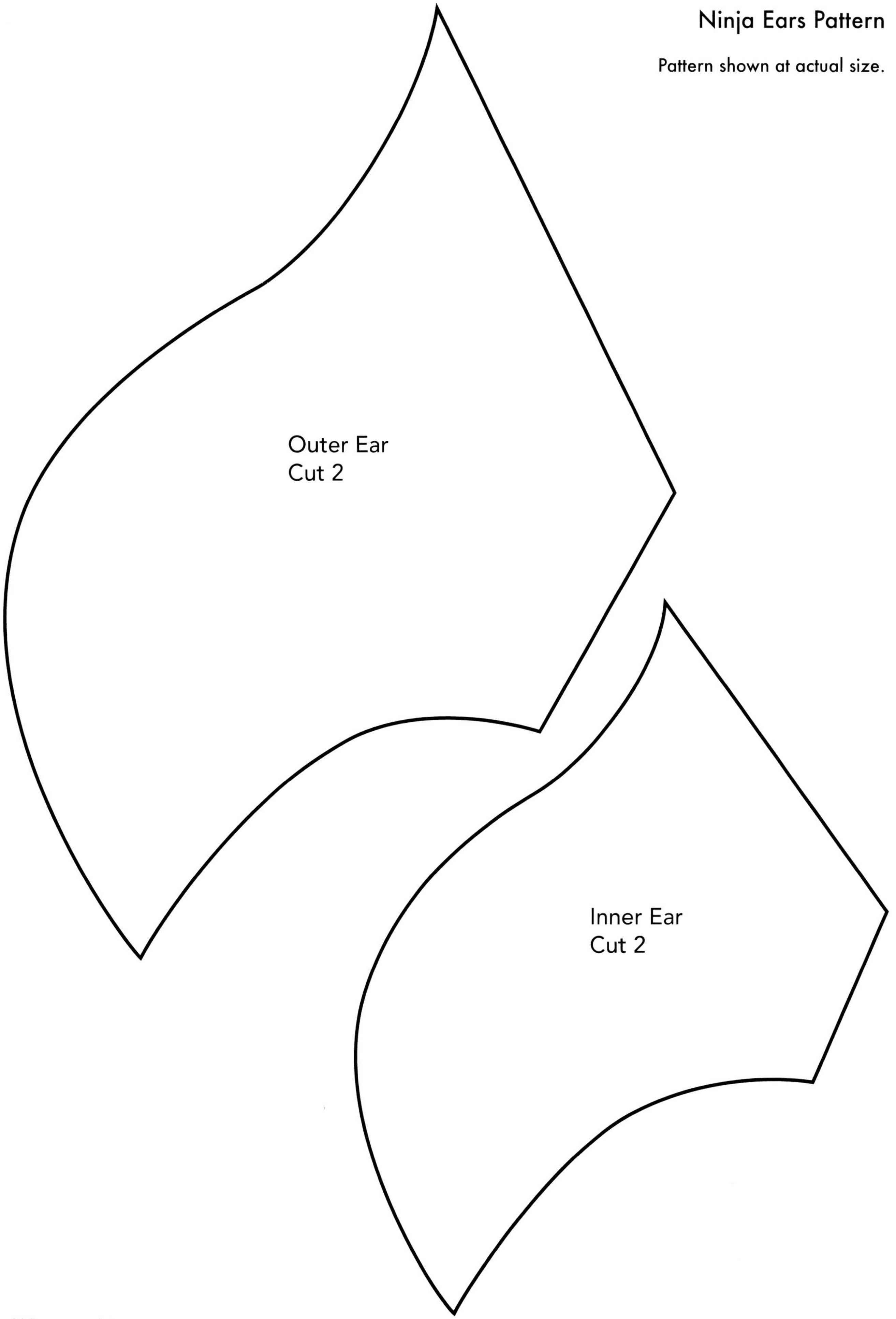

Pickaxe Pattern

Photocopy at 220% for actual size.

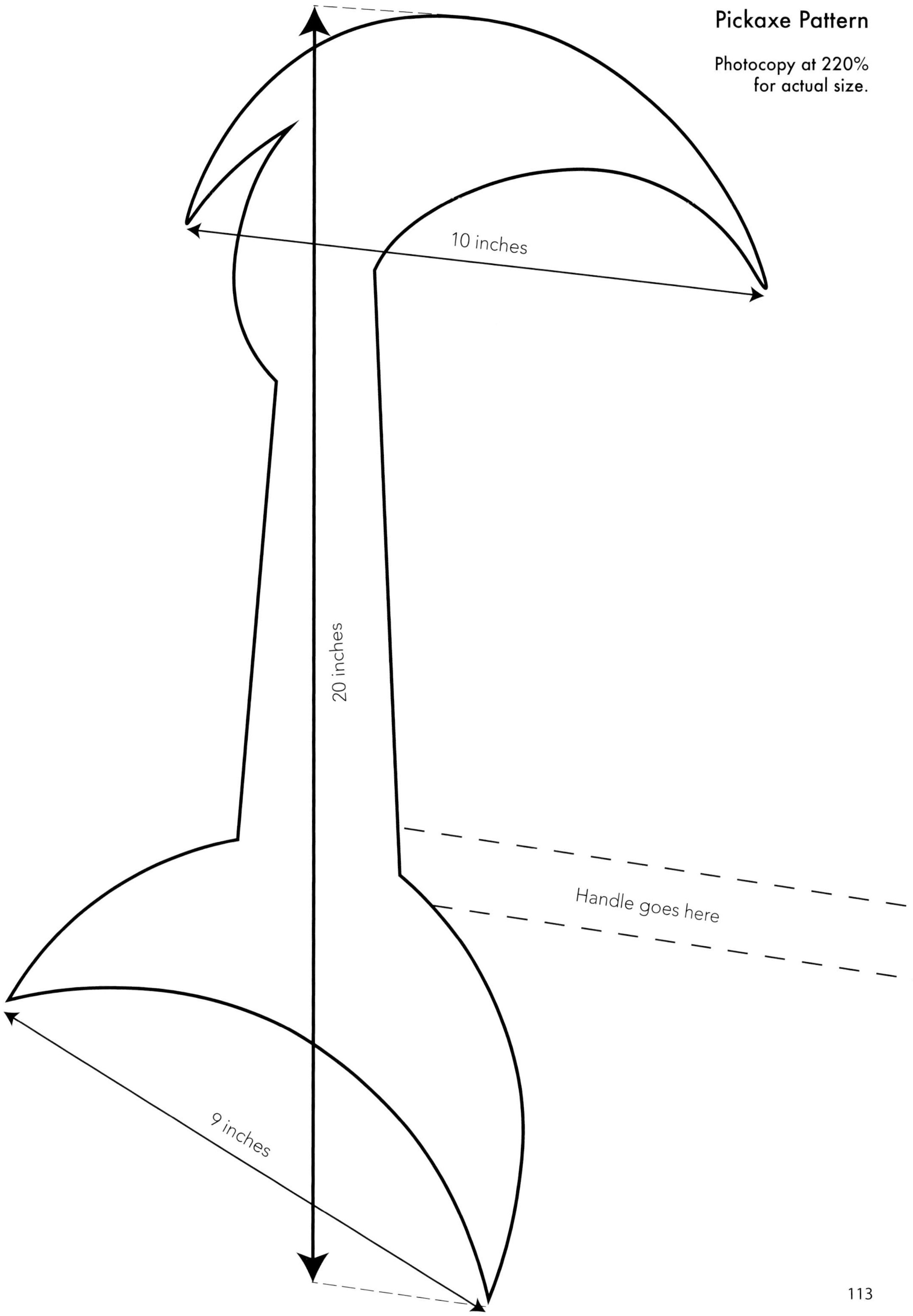

Pauldron Bodice Pattern

Photocopy at 400% or at size needed for cosplayer.

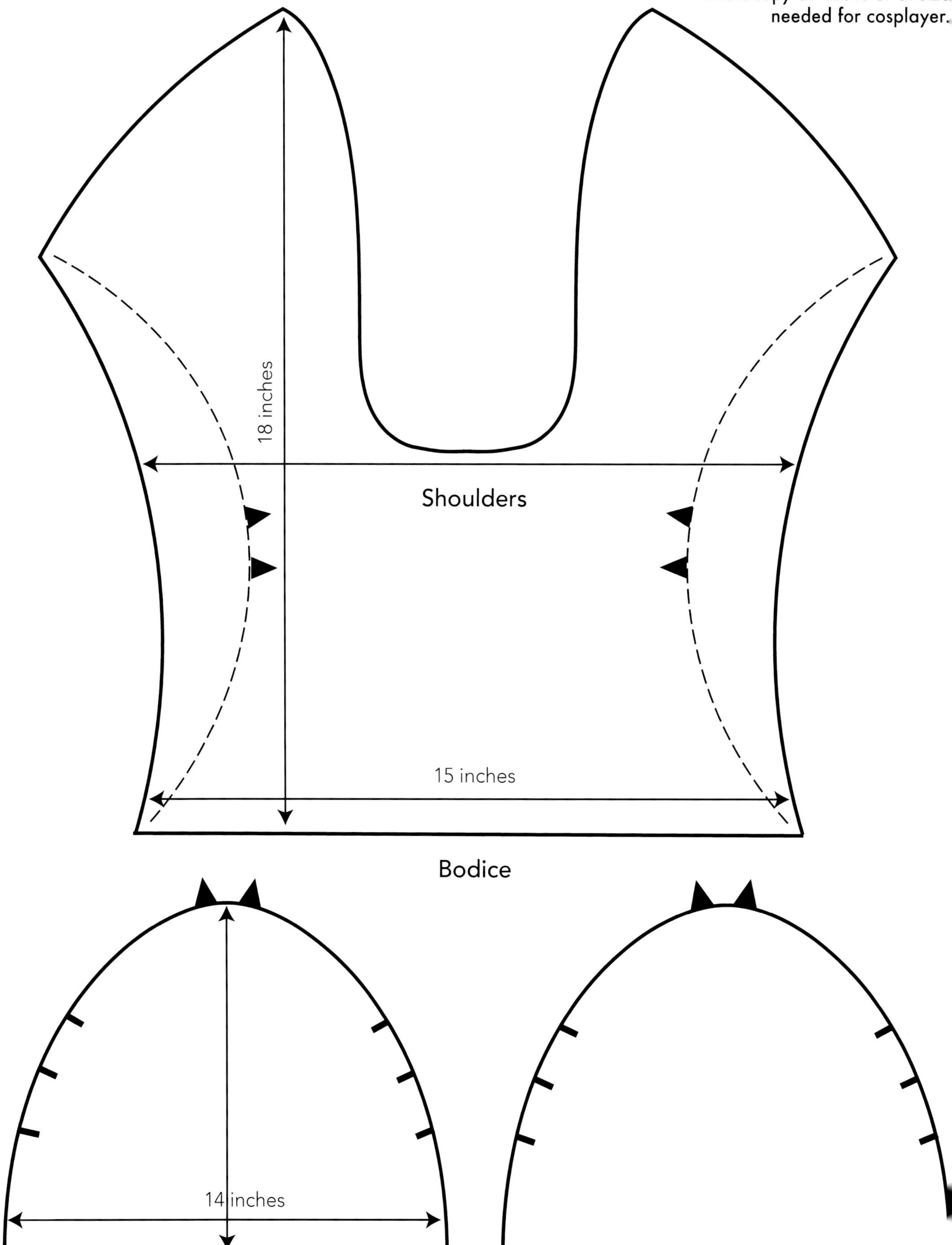

Shark Tooth Stencil

Pattern shown at actual size.

Croquis Sketchbook

This section of the workbook is where you can sketch your own designs, keep track of ideas, jot down your body measurements, attach fabric swatches, and use the book as a tool to build your costumes. Aspiring and established designers alike use croquis to sketch their costumes and garments to create the right proportions. Not only are they a timesaver, croquis templates ensure that your focus is on the garment or costume instead of the figure.

The word croquis (pronounced kro'key) comes from French and simply means to "sketch." In fashion, the term refers to a quick sketch of a figure with the clothes that are being designed. The croquis is a mannequin on a page. The croquis form can be "dressed" with any costume sketch you create. A simple pose is ideal, and that is what is included for you here.

You may want to use more than one croquis to develop your design: a croquis with measurements, a construction croquis, and a final croquis with sweeping designs and color to capture the entire vision. If you can imagine a costume in your mind or have a character you want to recreate, this workbook is here to help you draw and plan your cosplay to perfection.

The Art of **Croquis Design**

Model. Choose to work from either the male or female croquis outline that has been provided on the graph pages that follow. The proportions have been specifically drawn in a size that you can adjust larger or smaller to match your muse.

Measure. Use a flexible tape measure to measure the cosplayer and write down the measurements in the space provided on the croquis. These numbers are vital as you will use them when transferring the patterns for cutting out fabric and foam to make your costume.

Design. Build your cosplay sketches by adding the clothing to the croquis outline. A simple outline of the different pieces such as a skirt or cape will do. Use images of the character you want to become to sketch the shapes of the garments that you want to create.

Construction. Add general construction designs to the sketch. Indicate where zippers and stitching and gluing will be with dotted lines. This process may take a little practice, but it will help you make decisions for sewing, fabrication, and assembling the pieces.

Texture. Add texture and movement by adding things like pleats, folds, textures, and gathers to the design. Pleats and folds should be slightly darker and shorter at the fold line. Uneven lines suggest fullness and gathers. Patterns should follow the shape of the garment.

Color. Use colored pencils to build a color story after you have done your sketch. Use the color palette cues from a character you are recreating, or experiment with colors that resonate with you for a unique color story.

Views. You can include the back view and the inside of the garment. The back view can be a thumbnail image in the costume sketch. The underside of the design is typically identified with slightly darker shading.

Details. Make notes about substrates, trim, paint, foam, shopping, accessories, and anything else that will put the finishing touches on your costume.

Creativity. Unleash your passion for cosplay on every page of your croquis sketchbook. You will be amazed at the creative ideas that will emerge as you practice your skills and build confidence in your unique cosplay designs.

Design **Tips**

Start collecting magazine clippings and print out images of costumes that inspire you. Use them as ideas for sketching, positioning, shapes, and patterns.

Gather swatches of printed fabric and paint chips, then staple them to the page for reference and color matching.

Scan your croquis pages or take photos with your phone and pin the printed images to your inspiration board to guide you as you build your costume and for a quick visual reference.

Practice makes perfect. Sketch every day, honing the art of taking what is in your mind and seeing it come alive on the pages of your workbook. The more you sketch, the more you will see how easy it is to create designs that reveal the cosplay designer in you!

Made in U.S.A.

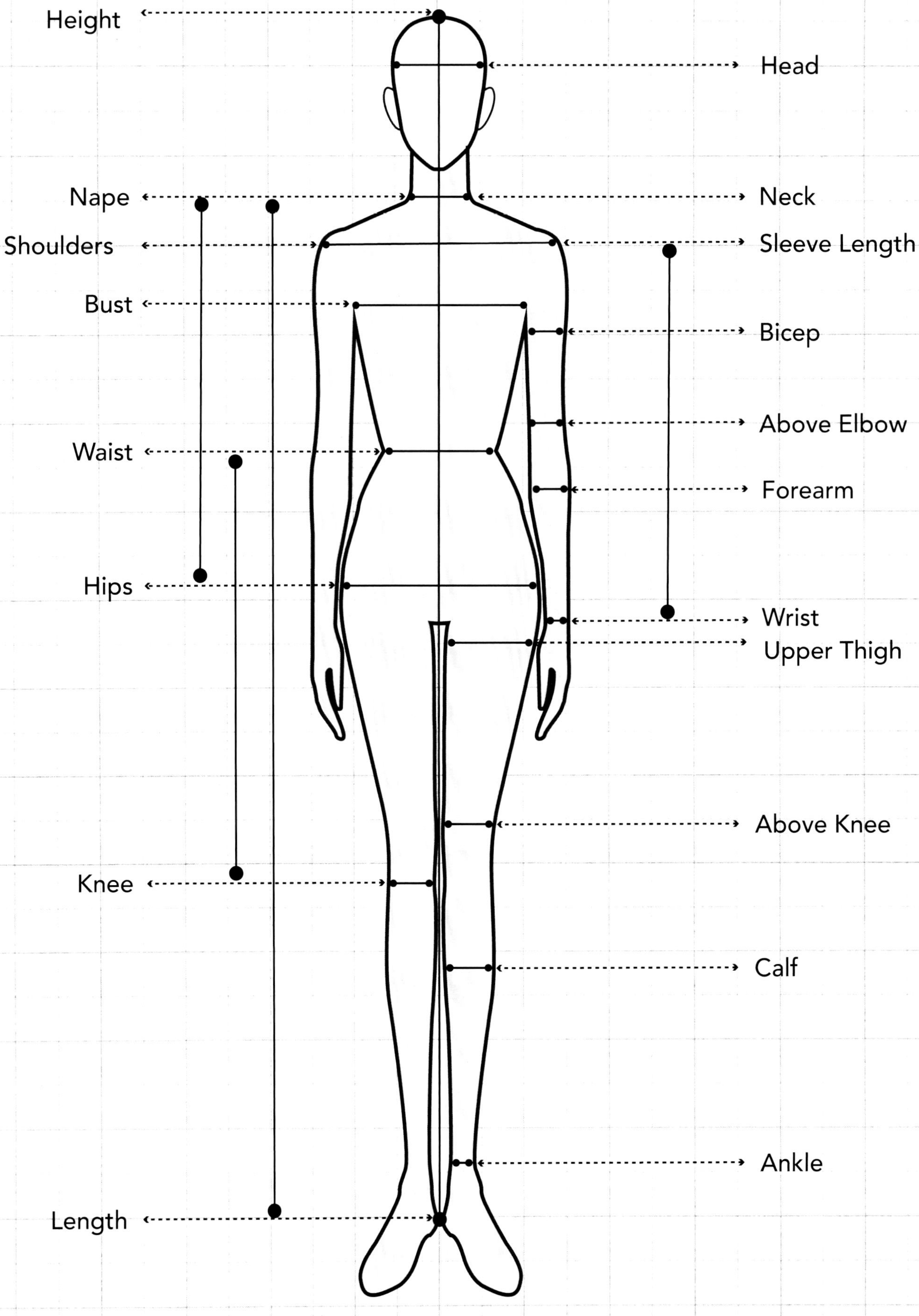
Height
Head
Nape
Neck
Shoulders
Sleeve Length
Bust
Bicep
Above Elbow
Waist
Forearm
Hips
Wrist
Upper Thigh
Above Knee
Knee
Calf
Ankle
Length

Female Croquis

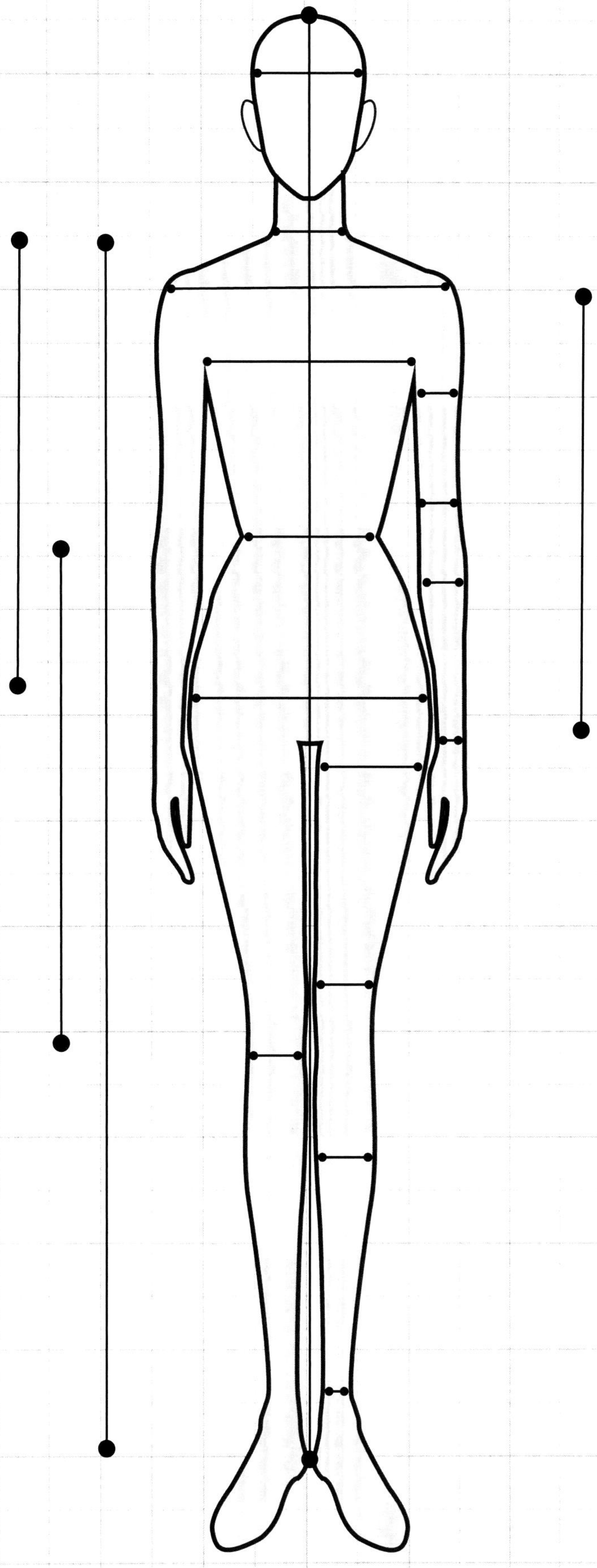

Female Croquis

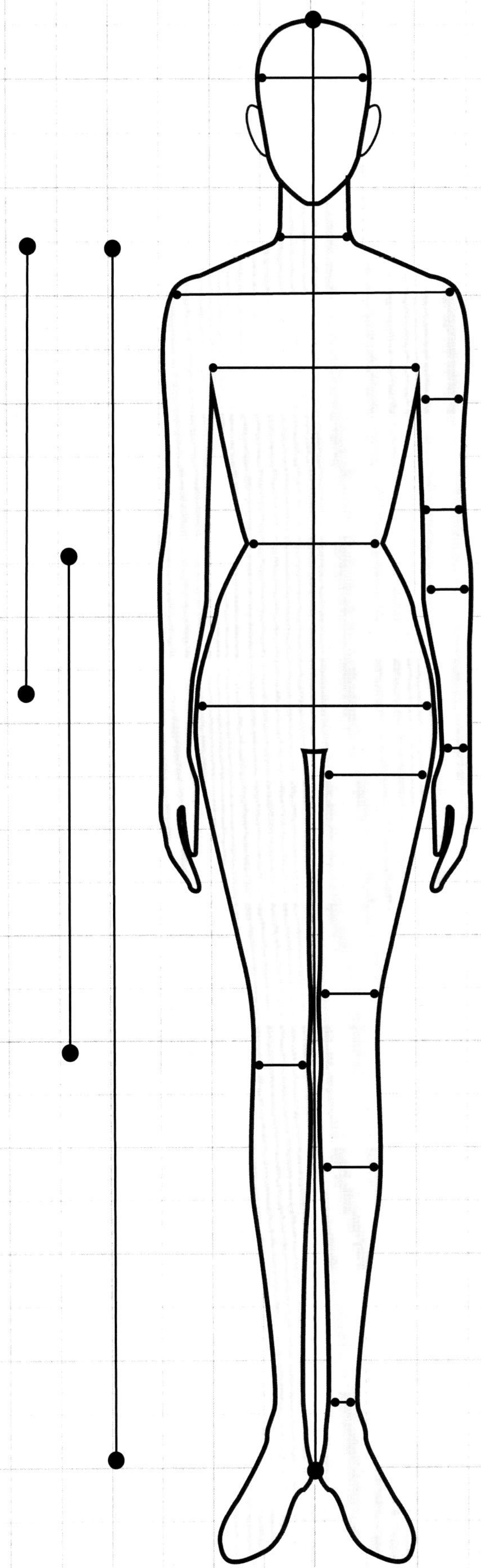

Female Croquis

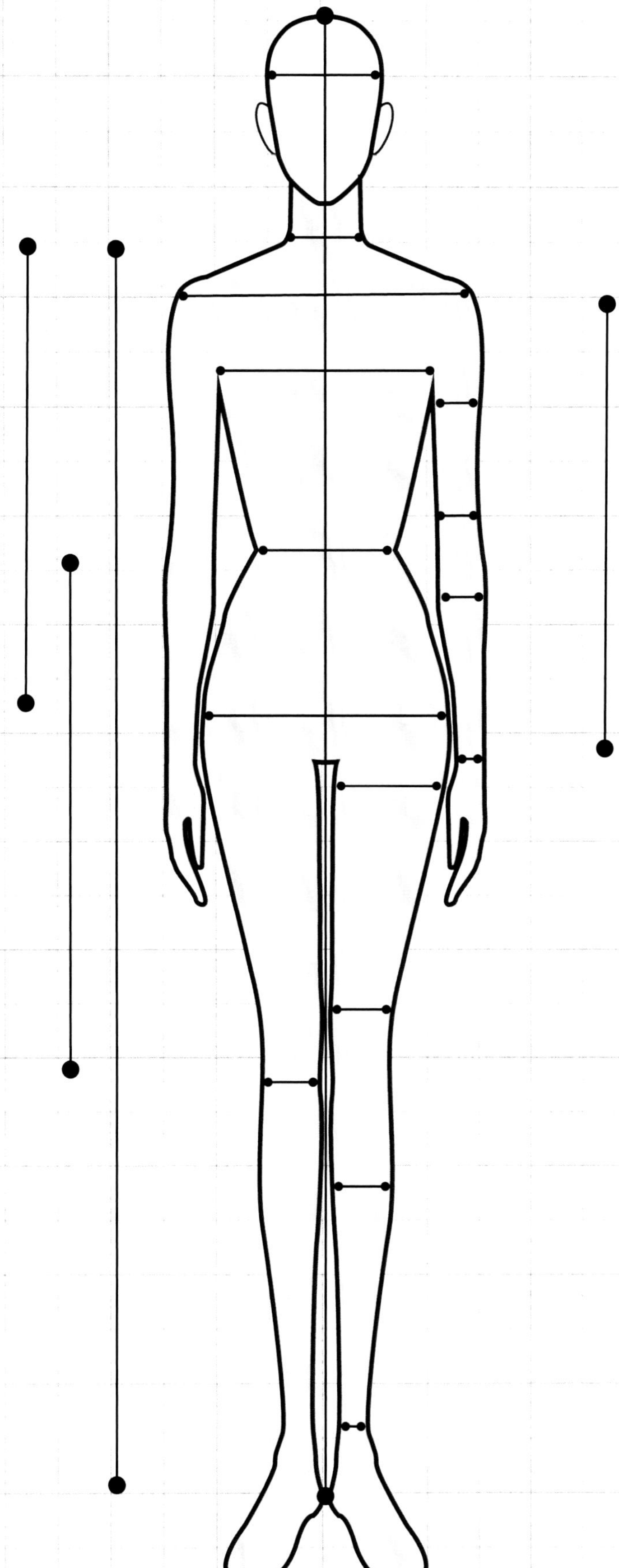

Female Croquis

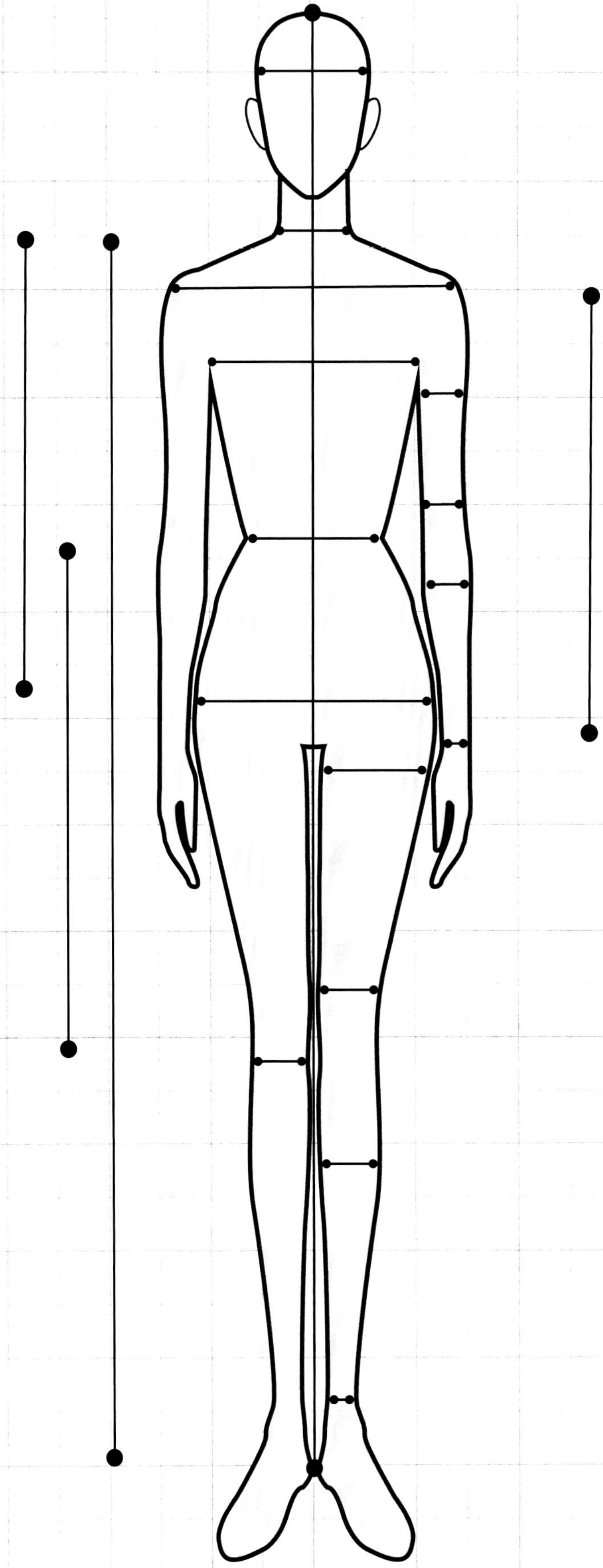

Female Croquis

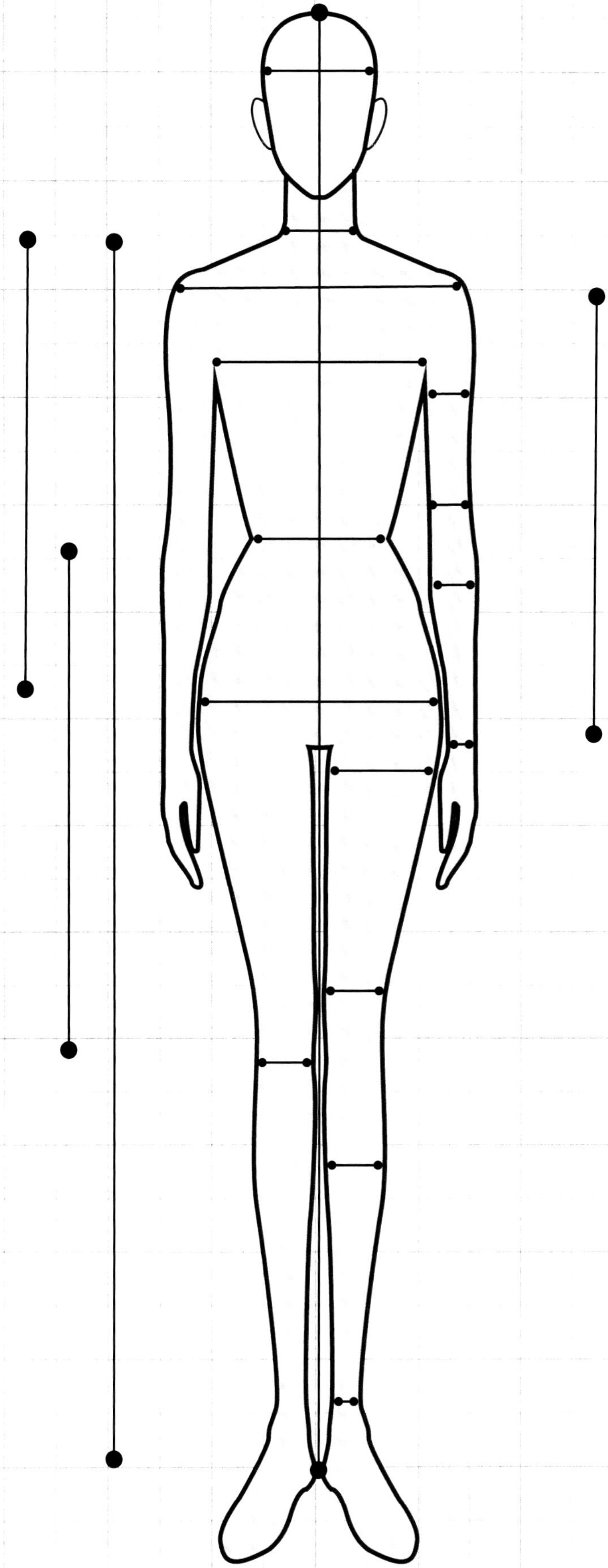

Female Croquis

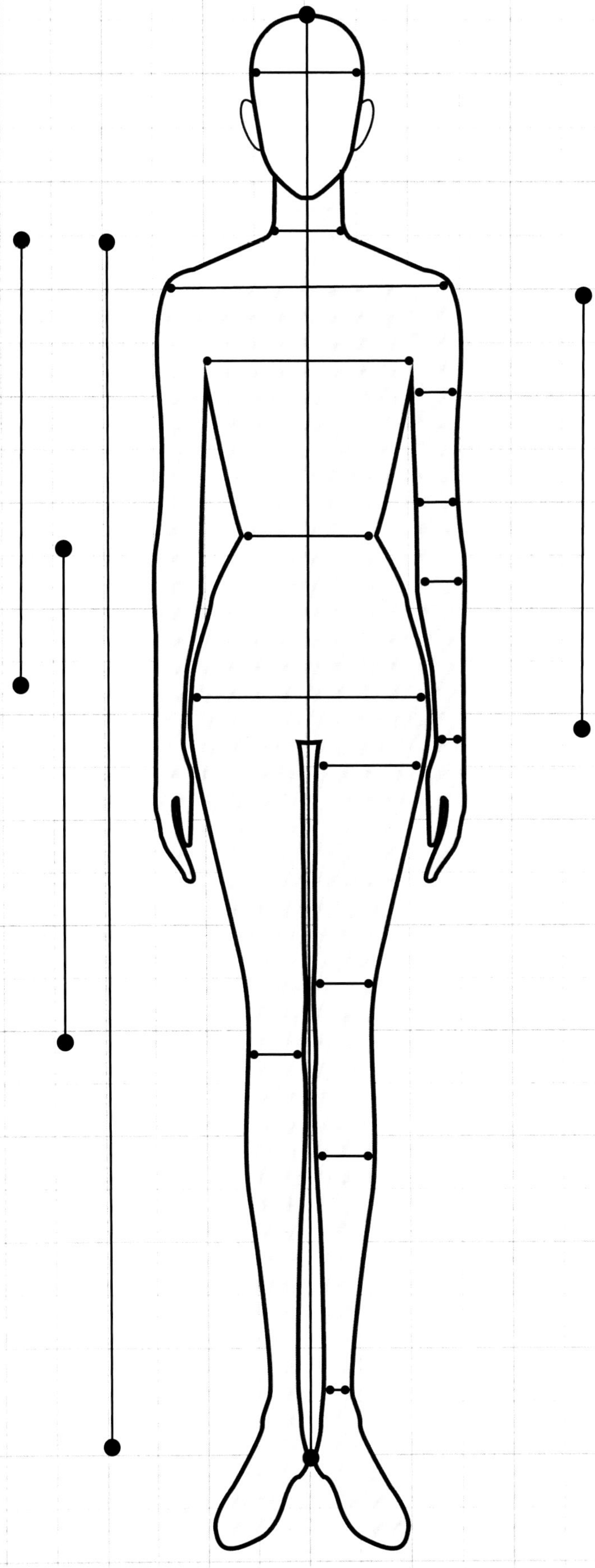

Female Croquis

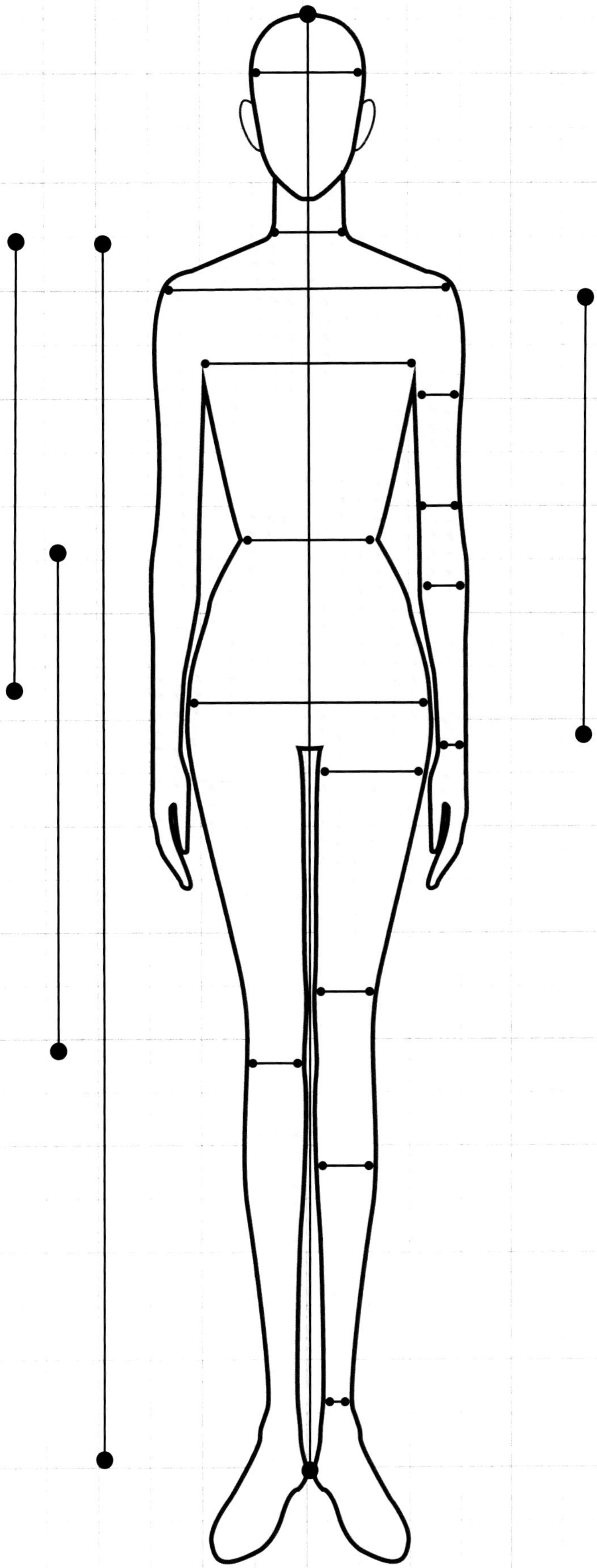

Male Croquis

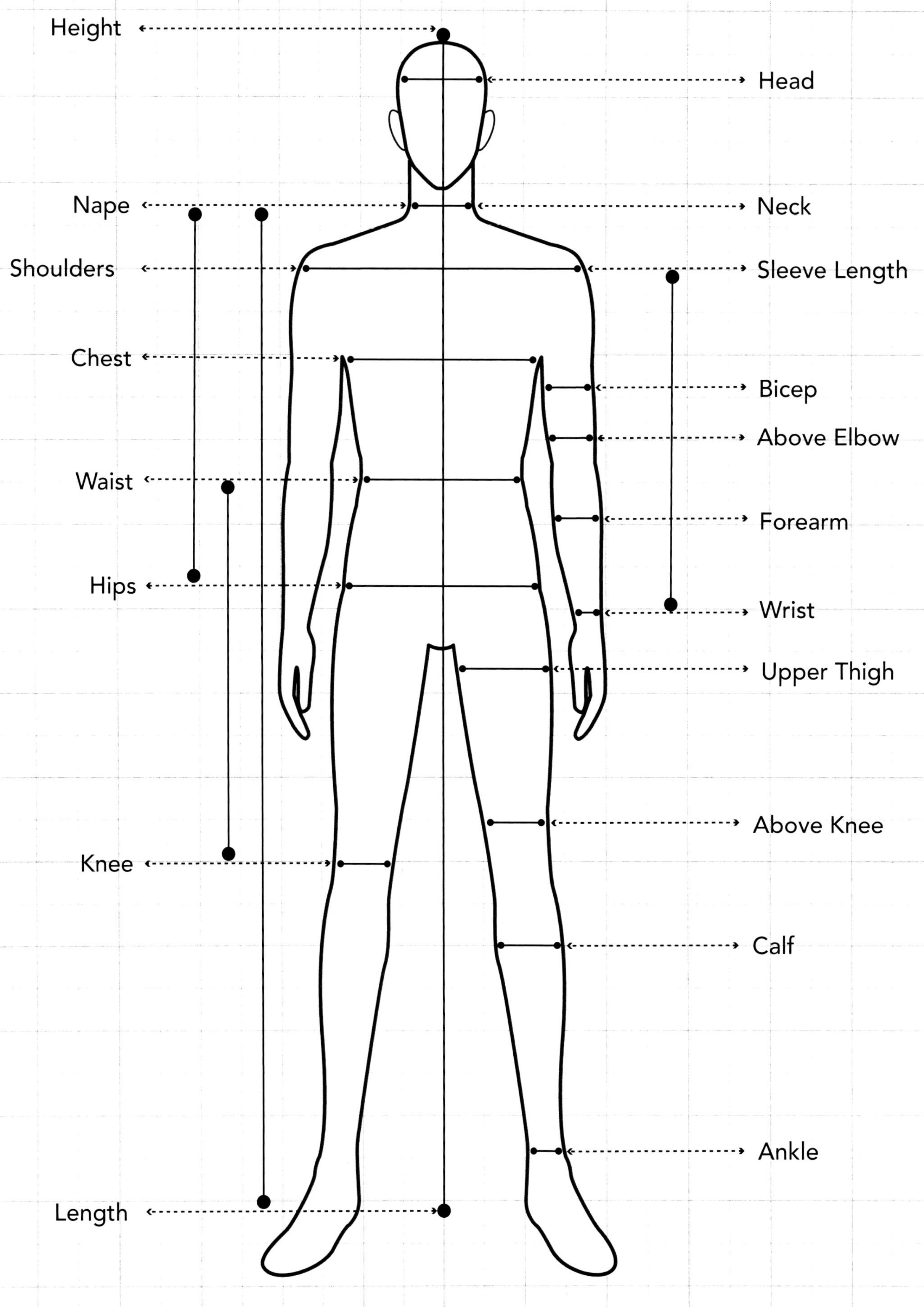

Male Croquis

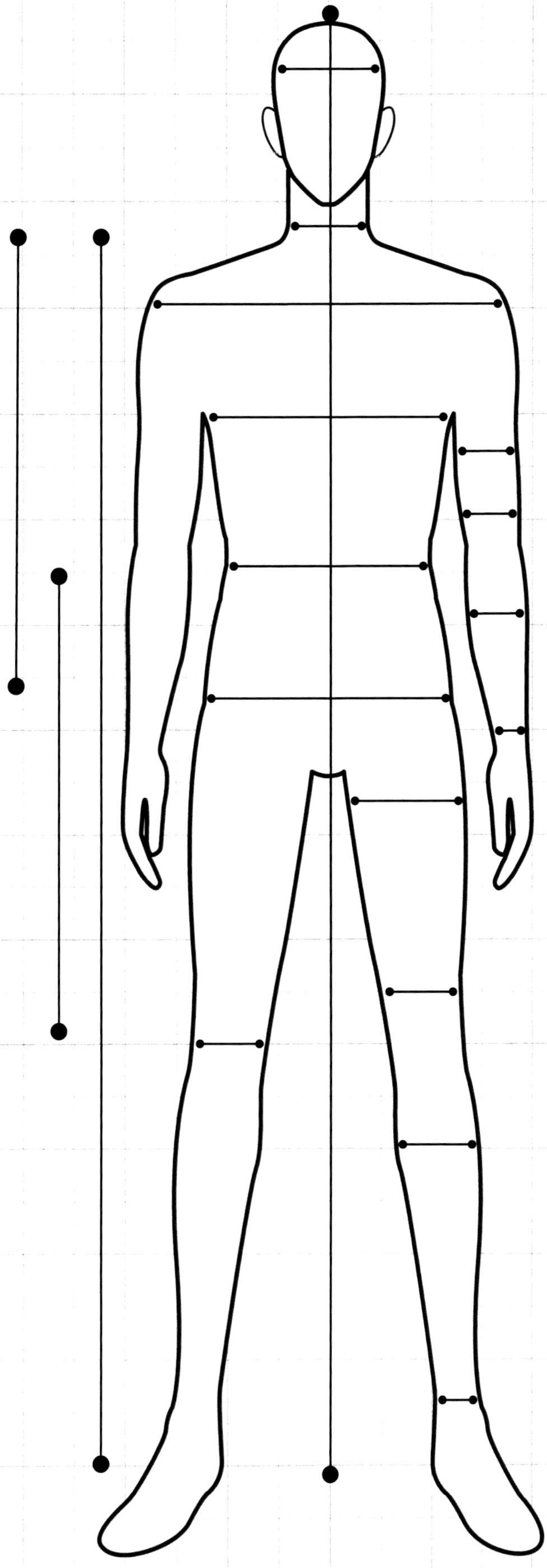

Male Croquis

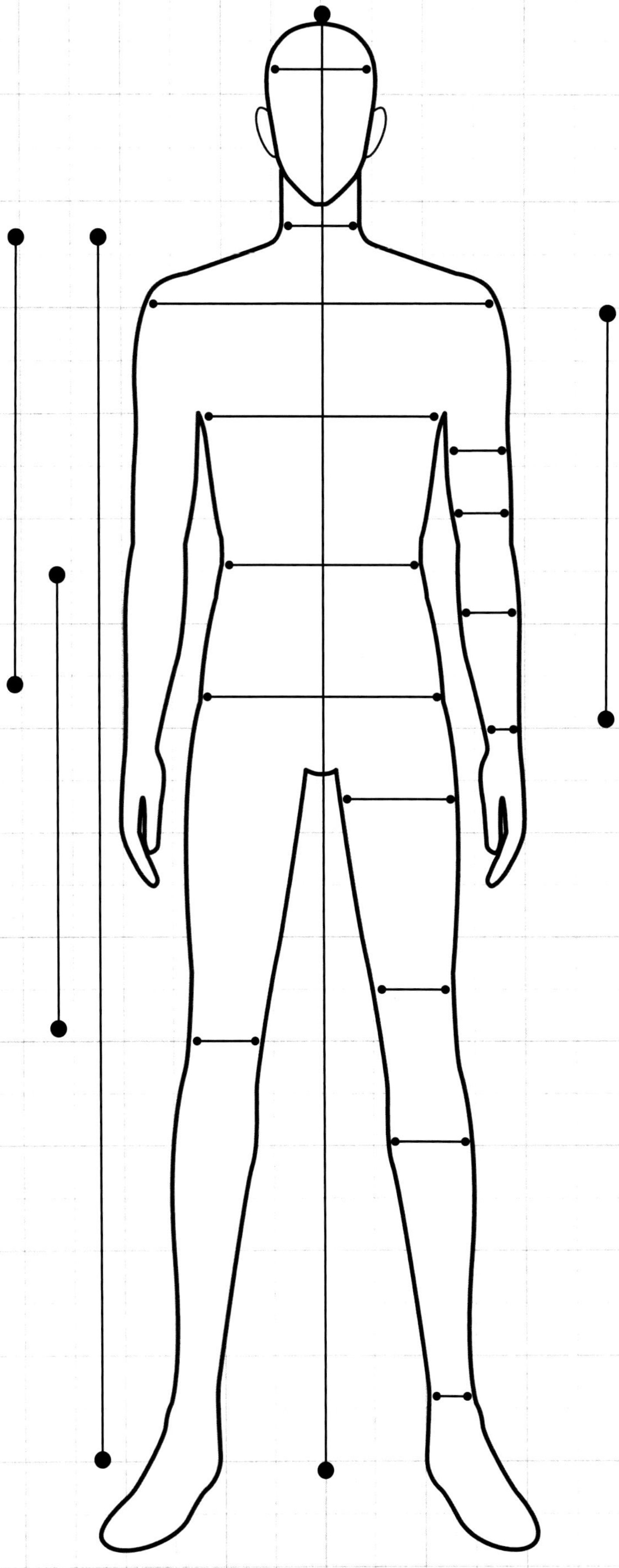

Male Croquis

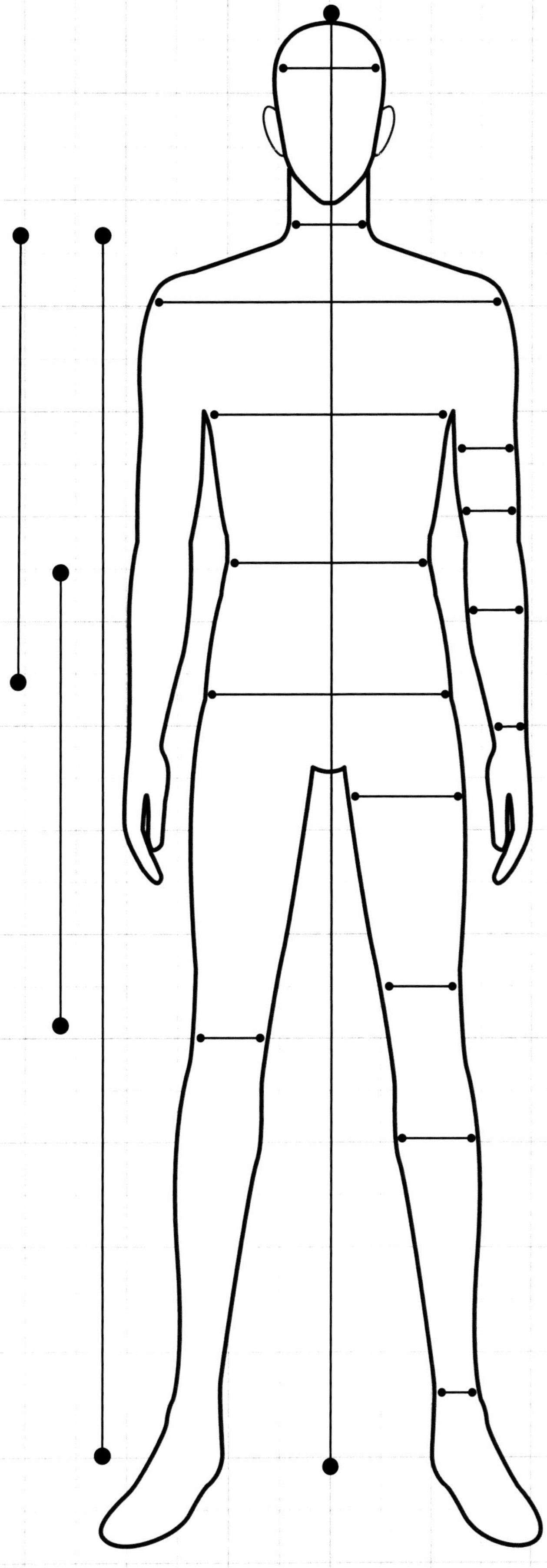

Male Croquis

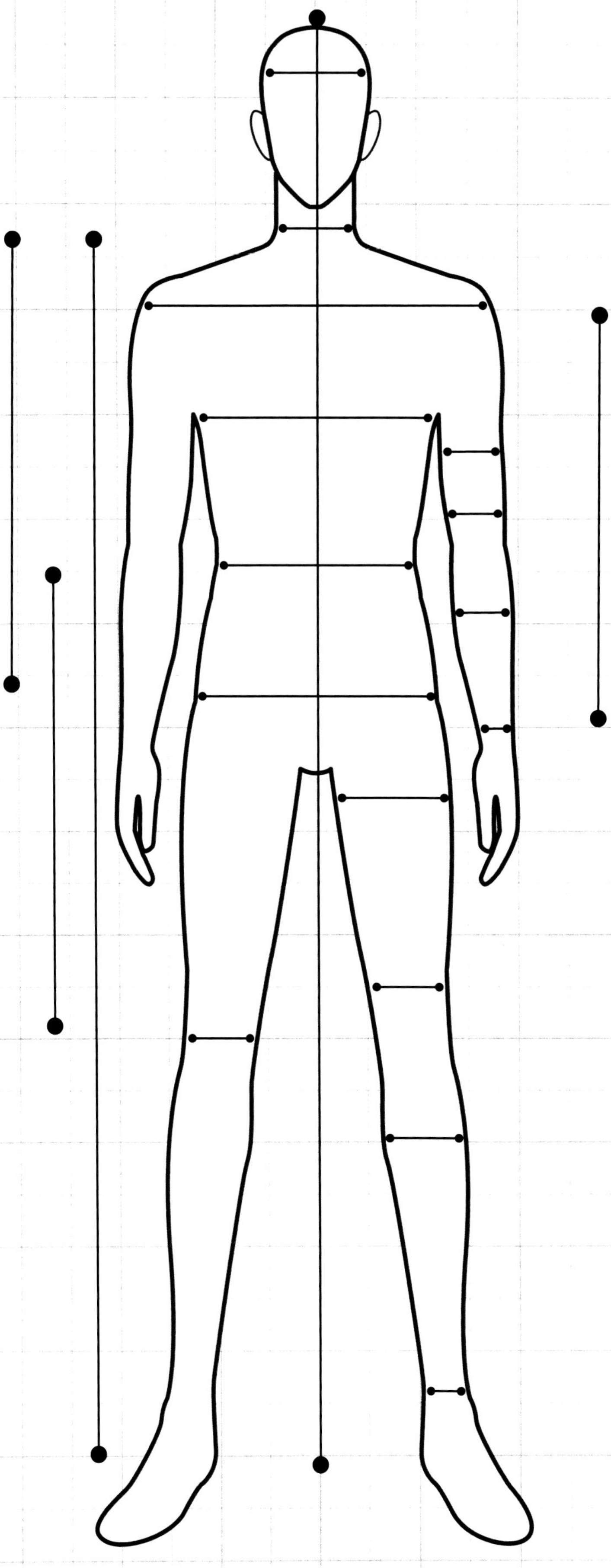

Male Croquis

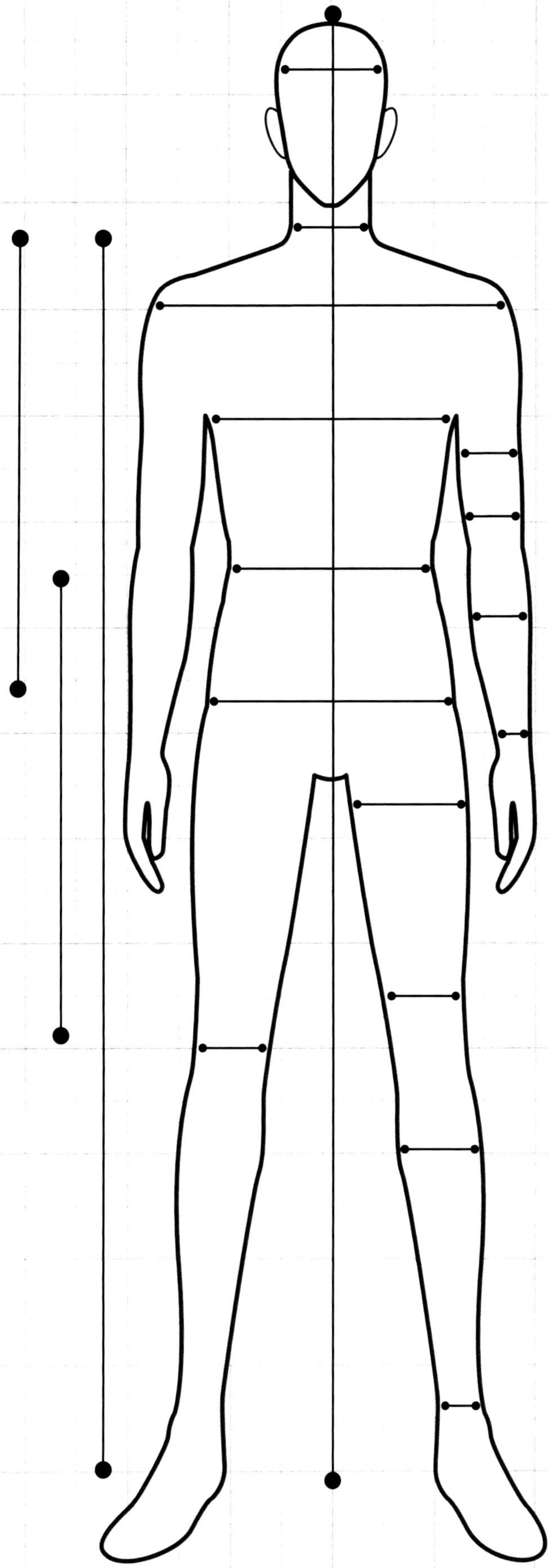

Male Croquis

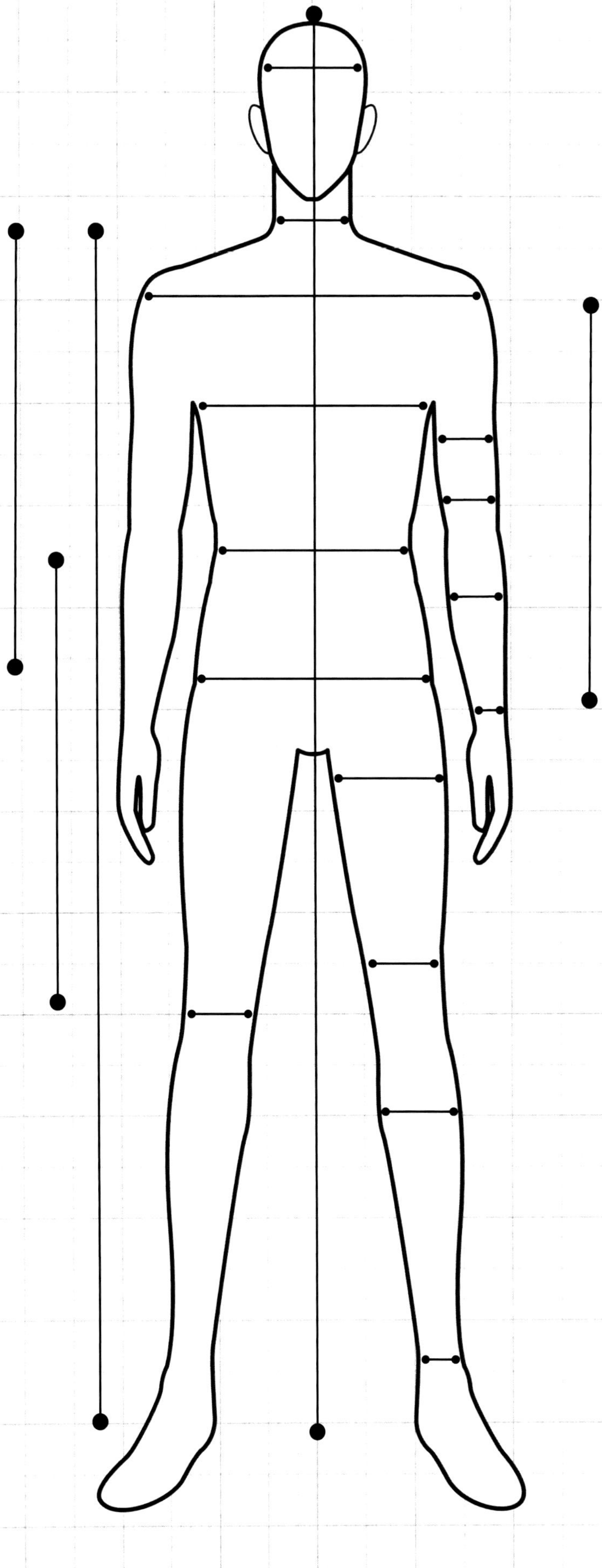

Male Croquis

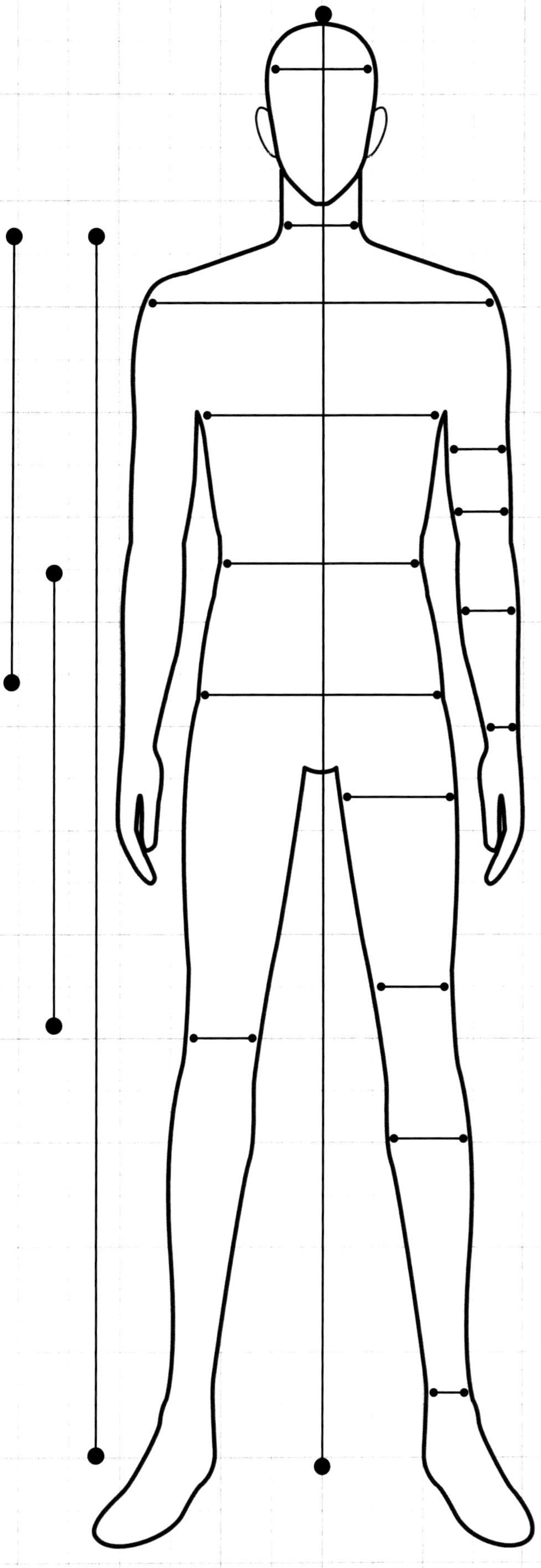

Acknowledgements

Thank you to my friends and family who are sharing this artful journey and who encourage me to reach for higher levels of creativity than I thought possible.

For reasons too many to number, thanks to Scott for being a supportive husband and creative partner who inspires me every single day and without whose help this book would never have happened.

Thanks to Tona Jolly for her enthusiasm and to everyone at Leisure Arts for understanding my vision and bringing this workbook to life.

Big thanks to all the models, contributors, and manufacturers who provided their professional goods and services to make this book a success.

Models:

- Unicorn Fairy - Chloë Tatro
- Nordic Princess - Lauren Garza
- Woodland Fox - Annabel Berroya
- Lollipop Girl - Heidi Thatcher
- American Superhero - Jeremy Small
- Centurion Gladiator - Matt Jones
- Top-Tier Ninja - Bee Xiong
- Sea God - Tommy Guerrero

Hair and Makeup:

- Tattoo Junkee® Cosmetics
- Desiree Chenot - Hair and Makeup Artist
- Tommy Guerrero - Tattoo Junkee® Sales and Planning Specialist

Materials and Tools:

- Fairfield™ Poly-fil® Fiberfill
- Fairfield™ Poly-fil® Glass Micro Beads
- Fairfield™ Aluminor™ Quilted Material
- Fairfield™ Solarize Thermal Material
- Fairfield™ Stick™ Double-Sided Fusible Web
- Oly*Fun™ Craft Material
- Fiskars® DIY Precision Tools
- Aleene's® Adhesives
- Tulip® Soft Matte® Brush-On Fabric Paint
- ColorShot® Premium Spray Paint
- AdTech™ Drip-less® Glue Gun
- Prym Dritz® Sewing Notions
- Oliso® Irons

Contributors:

- Bee Xiong - Designer of the Top Tier Ninja's foam sculpted shoes
- Scott Wilkinson - Designer of the Centurion Gladiator's Morning Star weapon
- Peggy Kelly - Santa Paula Times Newspaper Editor/Publisher, Bio Contributor
- Chloë Tatro - Writer, Bio Contributor

The Cataloging-in-Publication Data is on file with the Library of Congress.

Production Team: Technical Editor – Katie Weeber; Graphic Designer – Kate Moul; Photo Stylist – Pattie Wilkinson (Pattiewack Design Studio); Photographer – Scott Wilkinson (Pattiewack Design Studio); Hair and Makeup Artist – Desiree Chenot (Tattoo Junkee Cosmetics)

Made in U.S.A.